I Choose Life

Spiritual Transformation...
Experiencing Heaven On Earth

by Bee Godskiss Daley

*I Choose Life One, Two, Three…
I Choose to Celebrate Be-YOU-tiful.*

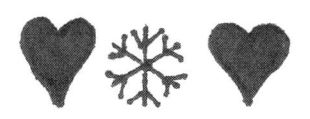

Copyright © 2013 Bee Godskiss Daley
All rights reserved.
ISBN: 1490565906
ISBN 13: 9781490565903

No part of this book or any of its contents, including graphic designs, may be reproduced, copied, modified or adapted, without the prior written consent of the author. The graphic designs are protected by U.S. copyright laws and are not to be reproduced, copied, modified or adapted, without obtaining written consent from the author.

DISCLAIMER:

I have tried to recreate events, locales, and conversations from my memories of them. In order to maintain their anonymity, I have changed the names of individuals and places in some instances, and I may have changed some identifying characteristics and details such as physical properties, occupations, and places of residence.

The author of this book does not dispense medical advice or prescribe the use of any technique as a form of treatment for physical, emotional, or medical problems without the advice of a physician, either directly or indirectly. The intent of the author is only to offer information of a general nature to help you in your quest for emotional, spiritual, and physical wellbeing. In the event you use any of the information in this book for yourself, which is your constitutional right, the author and the publisher assume no responsibility for your actions.

About the Cover:

The cover is a photograph of an art quilt that I made over a period of time. I initially made the figure in the center rising up in celebration with all of the butterflies around it because I had gone through a total transformation as butterflies do – from caterpillar to cocoon to butterfly – after I started going to Al-Anon in 1992. The middle figure is also similar to a phoenix rising up again after its life has crashed and burned. I selected *I Choose Life* as my title because that has been the major shift in my choice-making over twenty-one years of attending Al-Anon. The "one, two, three" has several meanings.

First, when I choose life, completely love and accept my uniqueness as a human being, I transform into a Be.You.tiful butterfly spreading joy to others. Second, when you combine chakras one (body), four (mind – see section on Chakras), and seven (spirit), these give you another one, two, three combination to focus on in your energy system. Third, when you focus on chakras one, two and three, you build the energy and strength to develop the other chakras and really blossom into who you were born to be. I like the play on words and how you can use the focus you want to start on this energy journey in your body. The swan in the far right corner represents another transformation from an "ugly" duckling into a Be.You.tiful swan with grace and ease. The snowflake with the heart around it, above the middle figure's head, reminds that there are over seven billion people on the planet, and no two people have the same fingerprint, just as no two snowflakes are the same. We weren't made to be the same but to be our own unique fingerprint in the world. The heart around the snowflake reminds us to love and accept whatever our unique human "package" is and to make the most of what we have to work with. The fish made of a painted seashell reminds us to go with the flow, because illness starts in places of constriction and stagnation in our energy flow. "De tout Coeur" means to put your whole heart into whatever you do. When we are able to integrate these pieces into our whole beings, we transform ourselves and help lead others; in so doing, we inspire others to do the same and show them the way by transforming ourselves and becoming artists of being *alive*.

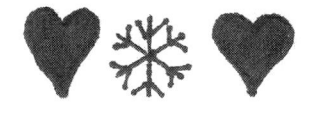

God's Kiss

This is an image I saw one day while I was meditating and it reminded me of the verse in Exodus 3:14, "And God said unto Moses, I AM that I AM" in response to Moses asking God what His name was. Since the original version of this was written so long ago, it is almost impossible to know whether the "AM" was really "AUM," and the translator changed it to "AM" because he did not understand "AUM." What if God was telling Moses that His name was "I AUM that I AUM"? Or what if it was written "I OM that I OM," and the translator changed it to an "A" to "I AM"? What if saying "OM" is a way of sending God's kisses out into the world? God created with His words, so this concept of creating and sending out God's kisses with our words or voices is fascinating to me. What if we taught our children to worship by sending out God's kisses to the world: "I OM that I OM" or just simply "I OM" or "OM"? In many religious traditions, there is a common belief that there is power in the name of the Lord (whatever name you have given the Lord in your tradition). Many yogis will tell you that meditation is the highest form of worship. What if these were the instructions for meditation/worship, and we misunderstood or didn't ever figure it out?

My favorite definition of *Namaste* is: The Divine love in me sees and honors the Divine love in you and when we are both in that place, we are ONE.

Acknowledgements

I want to thank everyone who has contributed to my healing and transformation over the past twenty-one years. There have been hundreds of people whom I have met through different Al-Anon and Alcoholics Anonymous meetings over the years that have contributed to my learning how to work the twelve steps and how to have a recovery that I am happy with.

I am grateful for my family of origin, all of whom have given me the experiences I needed to have in order to end up where I am right now. This is also true with my ex-husband and my children. I would have never gone to Al-Anon or kept going for so long without their influence in my life.

I am grateful for Sister Anne Winters and the Ursuline Sophia Center that provided many classes that have helped me on my journey.

I am grateful for Warren Grossman teaching me what it really means to be "grounded" and learning how that feels in my body.

I am grateful for Robert Moss and all of his dream work he has done for many years. Meeting Robert totally changed my life and opened fabulous and interesting new doors that have helped me create the life of my dreams.

I am grateful for Deepak Chopra and the Chopra Center teachers and staff, who also changed my life after I met them and experienced a weeklong workshop with them.

I am grateful to Linda Stone for the Artist's Portrait on the back cover of this book.

I am grateful for the many people who have encouraged me to write my story and to share it with the world.

Namaste

Introduction

I have gone through a complete transformation over the last twenty-one years, and when I run into people I knew when my children were little, many of them don't recognize me at all if they haven't seen me recently. As I have gone through this process, many people have told me they want to read my book to learn my "whole" story or have asked me when I would be writing a book about the transformation and healing that I have experienced. The complete irony of this book being "born" is that my ex-husband has been using many tactics to delay and drag out our divorce. After I figured out that my final divorce date had just been delayed another four to six months, I decided that it was time for me to write my book so I could make positive use of this extra waiting time instead of letting it get me really, really upset that I am still not done with my divorce and a lot of my life is on "hold" until the divorce is completed.

The other really interesting thing that has happened through this divorce process going on much longer than I initially expected is that I have had so many "gifts" from the universe come to me exactly when I needed them. There have been some incredibly kind people who have truly been "angels" in my life because of the help and support they have given me. I have had a number of people meet me for the first time and not believe that I am going through an ugly divorce because I look "great" to them—one of them was a divorce attorney! After that happened, I realized that I am capable of experiencing happiness and blessings whether there is turbulence from my divorce around me or not. I don't want to pretend that my divorce has not affected me or caused me any pain because it has.

Yet because of the tools from Al-Anon, meditation, yoga (including dream yoga), and ayurvedic lifestyle management, I am able to have a lot of peace deep within me and have had an amazing past year apart from the very real financial challenges in my life. Then it dawned on me that I was and have been experiencing "*Heaven on Earth*" in spite of the financial challenges created by my divorce. I could wake up and feel happy for no external reason at all and look forward to the day ahead of me to see what magical things would happen. Then I realized that we are all capable of experiencing "*Heaven on Earth*" every day once we individually have discovered the tools that work for us. I believe that the experience of "*Heaven on Earth*" is the same thing as the serenity promised in the Serenity Prayer and the "peace, which passeth all understanding" (Phil. 4:7) promised to us in the Bible.

My book has been met with a lot of enthusiasm from different people whom I have told about it, and it has helped me to "detox" by writing about my story. I have known for a very long time that I would write a book one day, and now it has actually happened.

I went through a period of time about twenty years ago when I was chronically sick with my sinuses and didn't feel very good most of the time. I remember praying during this time to God and asking, "God, please, if you will help me figure out how to feel better then I will help other people feel better by teaching them what I have learned." It is very exciting to me that God answered my prayer with the best physical health that I have ever had in my life, and, along the way, I have gained the tools and knowledge to be able to share what I have learned with others who are interested in healing and really transforming their lives from a place of sickness and illness into a life of vitality and abundant health and wellbeing. This book is my sharing of what tools and things I learned that contributed to my regaining my health and being able to experience *"Heaven on Earth"* as well.

Looking back, in hindsight I can tell you that there have been many little changes along the way that have added up to big benefits over a long period of time. The three major things that have ended up bringing about the biggest changes in me over the last twenty-one years are: 1. starting a daily and consistent meditation practice (although I didn't know that I was doing this at the time), 2. consciously working on changing my thinking about myself and the messages I tell myself about me and my actions, and 3. getting grounded with daily exercise, a community of support, and consciously changing the way that I spend money.

I had no idea that these seemingly small changes would end up bringing about a total spiritual transformation in me that started from the inside out and has completely changed the way I look on the outside and the way I feel on the inside of my body. My original inspiration for making these changes came from attending Al-Anon meetings—which I viewed as a punishment when I started going to those meetings. I really didn't like that I had been "forced" to move to Cleveland from Washington, DC if I wanted to stay married to my husband. What I did not know then was that Alcoholics

Anonymous (AA) was started in Akron, Ohio (about an hour away from Cleveland), and is stronger there than anywhere else because of its original roots and beginnings starting there. I did not get what I wanted, but I did get what I needed because I had grown up surrounded by the effects of alcoholism and had absolutely no awareness of this until after I was in Al-Anon for a few years. We are very blessed in the Cleveland/Akron area to have many, many meetings to choose from depending on your schedule, compared to other parts of the country that might only have one meeting a week in a place that is a half-hour's drive away. Now I love going to Al-Anon meetings and the support, strength, and inspiration that I get from them. I cringe at the idea of what my life would have turned into if I had not been going to Al-Anon for the last twenty-one years.

In Al-Anon, we learn that we can only change ourselves, and even that is not as easy as it sounds. Some of the changes I have made have been as easy as getting out of bed in the morning, and some of the changes have been incredibly difficult and have required a lot of persistence and perseverance on my part to keep working and moving in the direction I wanted to go—even if it felt like my progress was slower than a snail sometimes. There is a Rumi quote that says this perfectly: "Yesterday I was clever, so I wanted to change the world. Today I am wise, so I am changing myself." (1) The symbol for my Al-Anon home group is a butterfly, which is another symbol of a total transformation—from a caterpillar crawling on the ground to a cocoon to a beautiful butterfly flying around.

In the Al-Anon reading before the meeting starts, there is a statement: "Take what you like and leave the rest." Over the last twenty-one years, this has become another guiding principle for me in making choices, especially when I learn about something new or meet a new person. This concept was especially helpful for me with my kids when they were teenagers and complaining about doing something new that they didn't think they were going to like before they even tried it. I would encourage them to keep their focus on what they liked, and, after we were done, I would ask them what they liked. I didn't even ask about what they didn't like, and this helped keep things much more positive instead of having them get upset with me or complaining for a long time about something I made them try that they didn't like. I encourage any of you reading my story to take what you like and leave the rest. If even one small piece of my story helps you then I am glad that I could offer you something to help you on your life's journey.

I basically learned that I always have choices about everything around me and over the thoughts I want to nurture in my mind. I can use my choices to nurture and support life or to destroy life, and that is where I got the inspiration for the title of this book. A friend of mine told me that I had fallen in love with myself, and because of that, everyone else loves me too. What I did not realize until just recently is that when I make life-giving choices for myself, I end up being "Be.YOU.tiful" from the inside out and able to radiate this life-giving energy to others around me by the quality of my being and the way I live. The more I really love myself and love and accept living my life just as it is, the more "Be.YOU.tiful" I become. It is my goal to help everyone who reads this book to learn from my story how to cultivate this in their own lives so that they can transform whatever illness or crisis they are dealing with into an experience of health and vitality, abundant life, and wellbeing.

Namaste

Contents

About the Cover: vii
God's Kiss xi
Acknowledgements xv
Introduction xix

Chapter One — How Did I Get Here? 1
   Marie's Death..1
   Going to Al-Anon 8
   Turning Points..12
   Learning Who I Am 19
   Starting My Spiritual Practice 25
   Mother Teresa 32
   Discovering My Song.....................................36
   Learning about Who I Was Born to Be 38
   How Dick Got to AA......................................45

I Choose Life

Chapter Two — The Memories I Didn't Know I Had 55

 Healing My Heart 57
 Dealing with Resentment 64
 More Pieces to the First Memory 71
 More Memories 77
 Trying to Stay Alive. 83
 The Worst of the Traumas. 90
 Now the Odd Things Make Sense. 100
 My Destiny. 105
 Healing My Shame 107

Chapter Three — Healing Myself from the Inside Out 113

 Rediscovering the Artist in Me. 116
 Starting a Daily Journal 120
 Learning More about Mother Teresa 125
 Learning about the Bible. 126
 Many Different Bible Translations. 131
 Good Can Come from Suffering. 132
 God Talks in Our Dreams. 133
 Changing My Thinking. 134
 Singing My Song 136
 God Looks at Our Hearts 138
 Embracing the Beauty All around Me 141
 Being Conscious of the Choices I Make 142
 Developing My Unique Skills 143
 Becoming a Reiki Master 145
 Changing My Spending. 146
 Getting Grounded. 147
 Chakras and Colors. 152
 Discovering Dream work 154

Paying Attention to My Dreams..................................*155*
Dreams of Power..*157*
Honoring My Dreams..*158*
Past-Life Memories...*161*
Living with a Terrorist..*163*

Chapter Four — My Healing Really Takes Off............... 167
Going to the Chopra Center......................................*170*
Meditating and Didn't Know It.................................*172*
Chopra Center University...*174*
Financial Abuse...*177*
Financial Laws Need to Change................................*181*
Effects of Financial Abuse..*184*
Addiction—The Number-One Illness..........................*185*
Everyone Is Lying...*188*
Sexual Abuse...*190*
Teenage Suicide...*191*

Chapter Five — Consciously Choosing Life................. 193
The Guest House by Rumi(24)...................................*193*
Choosing Life..*194*
Working with My Chakras..*197*
First Chakra..*198*
Second Chakra...*210*
Third Chakra...*215*
Fourth Chakra...*220*
Fifth Chakra..*236*
Sixth Chakra...*243*
Seventh Chakra..*251*
Heaven on Earth..*257*

Abundant Life .... .258
Communities of Love .... .260
One Song by Rumi(50) .... .261

Appendix A — Pictures of the physical changes due to soul loss. 265

Appendix B — Positive Words and Traits 267

Endnotes: 281

Chapter One — How Did I Get Here?

Marie's Death

My journey started almost twenty-three years ago, the week after my daughter was born in June 1990. My mother was staying with me, and my sister Anne called my mom to tell her that my other sister, Marie, had found a lump in her breast and was going to have a biopsy shortly after my mother returned home to Virginia. My mom started crying while she was on the phone, and after she hung up, she told me what was going

I Choose Life

on. I remembered three dreams I had after Marie gave birth to a son, Drake, in January 1988. I had dreamt that I kept putting him in my car and taking him home with me. Initially, when I had these dreams, I had felt terribly, horribly guilty for subconsciously wanting to "steal" her baby away from her. Yet when my mother told me about the biopsy, I knew with very certain clarity that Marie was going to die, and I would end up adopting Drake after she did.

I had sinus problems almost from the day that we moved to Cleveland. I went to the doctor, and they tested me for allergies, and then I started getting allergy shots to help reduce my sinus infections. The shots helped me a little bit, but when I was still having problems, I got sent to an ear, nose, and throat specialist. He told me that my real problem was that I had a severely deviated septum and that I would probably have to eventually have surgery to fix it. Both Anne and Billy (my sister and brother) had deviated septums that were fixed with surgery, so I was not too concerned about this. Then the doctor asked

Chapter One — How Did I Get Here?

me when I had broken my nose. I told him that I had never broken my nose, and he looked at me like I was crazy. I had never done any sports or athletic events, and I never rough-housed around with other people as a child. I thought he was crazy for thinking that I had broken my nose.

After my sister Marie had her biopsy, we found out that she had stage-four cancer and she would be lucky to live another two years. This began the process for the rest of my family of working to figure out solutions for how to take care of her son, Drake, once Marie was no longer living.

My sister Anne thought she was going to adopt Drake when we first found out about Marie having cancer, and (unusually for me) I did not argue one bit about this with her but let her say whatever she wanted because I was pretty certain that it would work out for Drake to come and live with me. So after Marie had her biopsy, we found it was malignant (which I had known immediately from my dream), and her cancer was stage four. Marie was twenty-eight years old, and it had taken four doctors for her to find one that would give her a biopsy because of her age. She was scheduled for a mastectomy and then chemotherapy after that. Anne's daughter, Ruth, was the same age as Drake, and Anne was babysitting Drake a lot of the time that Marie was in the hospital for surgery and was going through chemo. My mom was taking care of Drake at night and on the weekends when she was home from work.

My husband and I had been married six years when I got pregnant with my daughter. My husband had always liked to drink more than I did but when I was pregnant with my daughter, I started noticing that my husband was drinking a lot of wine at dinner, sometimes almost two whole bottles by himself, but I did not know what to do about it, if anything. When my daughter was about eighteen months old, I was feeding her a bottle and watching a local show called *The Morning Exchange*, and they had a guest on speaking about alcoholism and how so many people didn't realize that it was a problem in their lives

Chapter One — How Did I Get Here?

and what the signs and symptoms were. That show on alcoholism awareness totally changed my life in a really good way. I realized that this was probably the problem with my husband and that there were a lot of high-functioning alcoholics like he was. I went to the library and checked out some books about alcoholism and kept them in the trunk of my car so my husband wouldn't know I was reading them. I became convinced from reading them that my husband had a problem.

In December that year, we visited my grandfather in the Northern Virginia area, and I went to visit my former boss Sterling Colton (general counsel at Marriott Corporation). Mr. Colton was also a bishop in the Mormon Church and was used to counseling people, so I talked to him about Dick and what was going on, and he recommended that I go to Al-Anon. He told me that he had seen many families have amazing results from going there.

In the meantime, Marie had gotten pregnant again (by the same man who was Drake's dad), and the doctors thought her cancer would not be estrogen-reactive and

I Choose Life

did not think it would be a problem for her to continue the pregnancy. The doctors were wrong, and her cancer took off with a vengeance, with her pregnancy hormones leading the way. Initially the doctors did not think Marie would live long enough for the baby to be viable once it was born. However, Marie hung in there, and when she reached twenty-six weeks in her pregnancy, the doctors at the hospital approached Anne, who was a nurse in the NICU (neonatal intensive care unit), and told her that the family needed to make arrangements to take care of the new baby since it was beginning to look like the baby would live once it was born. This was when Anne decided that she would be taking the newborn since the baby would be in the NICU, where Anne worked. This left Drake to go to foster care or come live with me. My two brothers, Billy and Joe, were not old enough or interested in taking on a newborn baby; Joe was twenty-two, and Billy was twenty-three.

I went to a counselor to talk about the issues involved in adopting Drake and moving him to Ohio from Virginia. I also talked to the counselor about the possibility of

Chapter One — How Did I Get Here?

taking both of Marie's children so they could grow up together. The counselor advised me that it would be too much to take on both of the kids at once, in addition to my own daughter, especially since Anne wanted the newborn and was starting to argue with me about how she would keep me from being able to adopt the baby. The counselor also recommended that I go to Al-Anon and that I could have a meeting with someone at a drug and alcohol treatment center to get help in dealing with my husband, Dick, and his drinking problem.

I made an appointment to meet with a counselor at a drug and alcohol treatment center, and while we were talking, he was writing down notes. I didn't know that he was filling out a questionnaire while we were talking. He told me, after about a half-hour conversation, that the questionnaire had twenty questions, and more than five positive answers meant there was a problem with alcohol. He told me after our conversation that I had answered "yes" to fifteen questions, and I felt like I was going to fall out of my chair. I had never dreamed that the problem going on in my house was so big. I also thought that alcoholics were the drunks under the bridge, and I now know that that is not true at all, and many alcoholics are very high-functioning in spite of their disease of addiction. The counselor told me he knew someone who went to a meeting with babysitting, so I could go during the day and not have to rely on my husband to babysit or try to prevent me from being able to go to a meeting at night.

Going to Al-Anon

So, in March 1992, I went to my first Al-Anon meeting on a Wednesday morning. I went to the beginners' meeting before the regular meeting started, and there were only four people there. There were almost fifty people at the regular meeting. I don't remember a single thing that the speaker talked about. I felt like most of the meeting was in a language that I totally didn't understand and really didn't have any idea what they were talking about. What I do remember is that people were happy and smiling, and I felt strongly that if I did what they were telling

Chapter One — How Did I Get Here?

me, things would get better. An old-timer gave me her phone number in case I needed help before the next weekly meeting. The babysitter gave me her phone number in case I needed babysitting outside of the meeting. I bought the two daily readers, *One Day at a Time* and *Courage to Change*.

I went home and started on the readings listed in the index in the back of the books, and I felt better. At the next meeting when I was talking to people about my dying sister, her son I was going to adopt, and my husband's drinking, people were very kind and sympathetic and always told me to "keep coming back." I felt like it was a punishment to be there, and I was hoping to only be going there for six months. I wanted to figure this out and be able to "fix" it and get on with my normal life. I still go to this meeting twenty-one years later, and it has totally transformed my life in ways I could never have imagined when I went to that first meeting. I had no idea of how good my life could be and how much I would like being me twenty-one years later. I can honestly tell you that Al-Anon is one of the best things that has ever happened to me.

After two or three months of my going to meetings and learning some little things I could do to help me with my husband and his drinking, my husband did not like the changes I was making at all! (And that is putting it mildly.) He was complaining and fussing so much that I was thinking about not going back to Al-Anon so he would calm down. Then one night after he had a lot to drink with dinner, we were doing the dishes, and he started muttering under his breath and complaining about everything. Then he took a steak knife and shoved it across the counter at me, and I realized in that instant that if I had not been paying attention, that knife would have cut me, and I could have been badly hurt. Right after that incident, I decided that I was going to keep going to Al-Anon no matter what because of how seriously injured I could have been by that knife. This was a big turning point for me because I was terrified of ending up divorced and having two little kids completely financially

Chapter One — How Did I Get Here?

dependent on me. I liked being able to stay at home with them, and that would not be possible if I got divorced and had to go back to work. I was hoping that Al-Anon would be my "cure-all" for fixing my marriage into the relationship I wanted it to be.

Al-Anon did not cure or fix my marriage, but it opened up a whole new world for me and gave me a lot of tools to use to deal with stressful and uncomfortable situations. It gave me a social network of people who understood completely what I was living with and were supportive and encouraging whenever I saw them. I didn't have to keep any secrets there or try to cover up the truth of what was going on in my house every day. I gained a lot of inspiration from all the people who shared their stories of experience, strength, and hope at the weekly meetings. Sometimes we broke up into groups, which gave me a way to meet people one on one, and that helped me a lot because I was extremely shy and quiet and afraid to tell the truth about what was going on in my house when I started going to meetings.

I Choose Life

In the opening remarks at most Al-Anon meetings, there is a line, "Take what you like and leave the rest." This has become a sort of rule for me that I use in all areas of my life so I keep my focus on what I like in any circumstance or place and with things or people I am around, and this helps me not to worry about the rest that I don't like. This has helped me over and over again in so many ways and seems like such a simple phrase, and yet it has rippled through to every area of my life and helped me to keep my focus positive.

Turning Points

One major turning point for me came when I was talking to an old-timer named Eve, and she told me she was giving me an assignment. Eve wanted me to make a gratitude list every day until I came back the next week, and she wanted me to have at least five things on my list every day. That night after my kids were in bed, I sat down to make my list, and I could only come up with three things I was grateful for. After about five minutes of trying to

Chapter One — How Did I Get Here?

think of two more things, I realized that my thinking was very distorted, and I had never been aware of it before. Then I decided I was grateful for peanut butter and jelly, and that gave me five things on my list. So then I worked at finding things I could be grateful for so I could tell Eve I had done my assignment. The really interesting thing was that as I found more things to be grateful for, the better I felt. I had no idea this would happen, although I'm sure Eve knew this, and that is why she gave me this assignment.

Now I still practice gratitude as a regular part of my days, and I can think of many, many things that I am grateful for. Sometimes I will pick a theme for what I am grateful for and think of things from every letter in the alphabet that I am grateful for or all the people at different meetings who have helped me over the years in Al-Anon or all the different types of food I am grateful for or an alphabetical list of things that make me happy. I have come back to my gratitude list many times over the last two years during my divorce, especially when I have very little money compared to my "normal" lifestyle of the last twenty-seven years. It still helps me and lifts me up no matter what else is going on.

Another big change came for me when I decided that I wanted to figure out how to pay off all of our debt besides our mortgage. My husband owned a successful business and earned a good income, and it was a mystery to me why we had so much debt, and he was acting like we had no money at all. This proved to bring me a lot of personal growth as I started doing without "extras" that had just become habits for me. It took almost two years, but I managed to pay off all the credit card debt we had and even saved some money in a savings account. When my husband found out about the saving account, he flipped and started yelling and yelling about how we didn't need a savings account since we had the business to take care of us financially. What I know now is that he didn't want me to have that savings account because he wanted total control over our finances. He even managed to rack up all of the debt again that I had worked

Chapter One — How Did I Get Here?

so hard to pay off, and I realized that I would never be able to pay off the debt as long as I was married to him. This was one of the factors that made me realize that my relationship was not nourishing for me, and it was time for me to let go of our relationship that was no longer "serving" me or nourishing me. Nourishing choices always feel comfortable and bring out the best in us so it was pretty obvious to me that our relationship was not bringing out the best in me at all. Spending time alone with my husband stopped being enjoyable and comfortable a long time ago.

The next thing I worked on was figuring out how to stop arguing with my husband all the time. No matter what, he was turning everything into an argument. I do not like to argue, and it was really driving me crazy that he kept picking fights with me every time I turned around. Then I heard a speaker at a meeting talking about how she handled the difficult people in her life now compared to how she used to deal with them. She said she would take her daily reader and go into the bathroom and read about topics that would help her at the time. After she had calmed down, she would leave the bathroom, and because she had "changed" where she was mentally then the argument or difficult situation would be changed because she had changed her mental outlook. I remember saying to myself, *I can do that the next time he picks a fight with me.* I put one of my daily readers in the drawer in my bathroom (I still have a copy there today), so I would be ready the next time he tried to pick a fight with me. It didn't take very long for him to pick a fight, and he was yelling at me for something (so important that I don't even remember the topic—only the yelling). I remembered my book in the drawer and told him I needed to go to the bathroom. I went in there and read for almost twenty minutes because I was shaking all over my body. When I walked out of the bathroom, he looked at me like "What the heck just happened?" The fight was over, and I felt really happy that I had found a way to turn this situation around. We got to the point where those arguments never happened again.

Chapter One — How Did I Get Here?

I have a friend who wrote down scripts of appropriate and positive things to say during difficult situations that she kept in her pockets so she could pull them out and read from them when she got into an argument that she didn't want to engage in. She has a script to use with her kids in one pocket and a different script to use with her husband in the other pocket.

I started exercising on a regular basis, which was something I did not learn growing up because my mom and family didn't really pay attention to exercising at all. After a few weeks of exercising three times a week, I started to notice that I felt a lot better after I had just worked out, so I kept up with this routine. Then when things got really stressful at our house, I started taking walks outside in our neighborhood to calm down and shift my thinking to a better place. This is a habit I still have twenty-one years later, and many people in my neighborhood will come up to me in stores and restaurants and tell me they know me as "the walker." This has been one of the best changes that I ever made, and I look

I Choose Life

forward to my daily walks. I was happy when I started learning about ayurveda (ancient healthcare practices from India) and learned that walking after you eat is good for your digestion and wellbeing.

Then I decided that I needed to work on developing better eating habits because in my house of five children, my mother had enough other things to do and didn't care what we ate as long as we weren't starving. So if you wanted to eat chocolate cake for breakfast then that was fine with her. I also grew up in the South, where there is a lot of fried food, and my mom cooked a lot of fried food too. It was major growth for me to realize one day that French fries didn't taste good to me anymore, and I remember thinking, *How did this happen?* Now, as a Chopra-certified meditation instructor, I know that changes in your level of awareness also bring changes in the types of foods that taste good to you. The changes in my eating have definitely had a good benefit on my body and overall wellbeing. Now I am very in tune with my body and the effects that certain types of food have on

Chapter One — How Did I Get Here?

me, either good or bad. I am much more conscious of the food choices that I make now than I have ever been in my entire life.

Learning Who I Am

I had joined the Junior League when I moved to Cleveland, so I would have a way to meet other women and have something interesting to do. I was at a Junior League meeting one night and heard a guest speaker who told a story that has stayed with me for twenty-three years (I was pregnant at the time with my daughter, who is currently two months away from her twenty-third birthday). This is the story she told us: There was a baby eagle that fell out of its nest and landed in the middle of a bunch of chickens on a farm. The farmer noticed the baby eagle but had no idea where it had fallen from and let it stay because the chickens were taking care of it. Over time, the eagle grew up, and it was hanging around with the chickens, pecking the ground for its food. The farmer noticed this one day and thought that it just wasn't right

I Choose Life

for an eagle to be acting like a chicken and decided that he would take it up on the mountain and let it go, so it could go back to its true nature of being an eagle. The farmer took the eagle up a little way on the side of the mountain and let the eagle go. The eagle took off flying very high, circled around three or four times, and then flew down to the farm with the chickens because that was its "home." The farmer was shocked that this happened and let the eagle stay there since it thought it belonged there. Then, one day, he decided he would try again to return the eagle to its natural environment, and he took the eagle up much higher on the mountain and let it go. This time the eagle took off flying and circled around about eight or nine times and then flew back "home" with the chickens. The farmer felt very surprised and frustrated that the eagle wouldn't go be an "eagle" and was pecking the ground like it was a chicken. After some more time went by, the farmer decided that he was going to try one more time and decided to take the eagle to the top of the mountain and then let it go. Once they got to the top of

Chapter One — How Did I Get Here?

the mountain, and the farmer let the eagle go, it took off flying very high, circled around many, many times and never came back again. The farmer was ecstatic that the eagle had finally taken off to be true to its nature of being an eagle.

The speaker was talking about how a lot of us were born "eagles," and different people in our lives had convinced us that we were chickens, and we believed them and weren't true to our natures because of it and also didn't fully develop our strengths and talents because of this. She was urging all of us to find the "eagle" within each of us and to work on nurturing and developing our true natures in order to benefit the world. I left that meeting and kept thinking to myself that I was an eagle, and my mom had been a chicken (her true nature), and I needed to figure out how to be an "eagle" again. I was thinking a lot of the time about how I was an eagle, and then my husband came home from work one day with business Christmas gifts he had received just because he owned his own business. He gave me these gifts and told me that if I wanted them, I could keep them, and if I didn't like them, I could throw them away because he didn't care about any of them. I opened a package, and inside was a beautiful, carved wooden eagle about a foot tall. My first thought was, *Oh, my gosh, I really am an eagle!* Then the skeptic in me started thinking that everyone probably got an eagle, and I made a mental note to pay attention to what my in-laws had gotten the next time we were at their house. The next time we were there, I saw that my father-in-law (who is also involved in the business) had received a carved wooden owl and not an eagle. Then I felt convinced that I really was an eagle.

I had never studied anything about Shamans or Native-American traditions and had no idea that the eagle is a sacred bird and a very spiritual bird in the Native-American tradition. I felt a little overwhelmed when I learned this because there was no doubt in my mind that I was an eagle because of the circumstances that led me to believe this, and yet I did not have the self-confidence to really own this as a personal symbol and totem. It has

Chapter One — How Did I Get Here?

taken me a long time, but I can own this wonderful bird as a part of my energy now and as my totem.

The next thing that I realized as I was going to Al-Anon was that I had "lost" who I was and wasn't really doing things I had liked to do before I got married. I used to love to read and had completely lost this part of myself to the disease of alcoholism. There are a lot of books in Al-Anon, so I started reading as many of them as I could, in addition to the daily readers that I was reading every day. It felt so good to start reading again, and I can tell you now that reading is a very nourishing activity for me.

Al-Anon encourages you to take time for just yourself on a regular basis to do something you want to do. It was incredibly, terribly hard for me to think of something I wanted to do all by myself that would be good for me. I finally came up with the idea of going to get my nails manicured every week because I couldn't think of anything else I wanted to do with the spare time on my hands. Now it seems hard to imagine not knowing what I would like to do with spare time, but it was excruciatingly difficult for me at the time because I was completely tangled up with my alcoholic and his disease and had lost myself so much that I couldn't think of things to do alone that I would enjoy. On one of the first vacations we took after my husband got sober, we were at a nice resort, and he told me to take a couple of hours for myself away from the kids. I had already gotten my nails done, so I had no idea what I wanted to do with myself. I ended up buying myself a pretty journal that had been locally made, and I went and sat by the beach and started writing in that journal about what was going on in my life. I learned as part of my training at the Chopra Center that journaling is a form of emotional detoxing, and my instincts about doing this had been good for me. This became a recurring theme for me as I continued to go back to Al-Anon—that my natural instincts are the most nourishing choice for me, and that it is up to me to choose to be true to myself and honor those natural instincts instead of letting other people pull me away from my true nature and what the best choices are for me.

Chapter One — How Did I Get Here?

Starting My Spiritual Practice

Twenty-one years later, I am much better at sticking with the choices that are the most nourishing for me, although this is still a challenge. It is particularly difficult for me if I am with a lot of people who are all on the same page, and I need something different than they do. I am much better at this now, and I remind myself of the Al-Anon slogan "progress, not perfection," so I don't mentally beat myself up when I am not strong enough to honor the best choices for myself.

When my sister Marie was dying, I went with my other sister, Anne, to see a psychic named Kelly. All I knew was that she was a retired minister who had started her own church, and she was in her eighties. She wanted to talk to me by myself, and she told me that I was here to walk on a spiritual path for this lifetime. She told me I was a "star child" from another planet and that I was here to help with the earth changes. She told me that I needed to raise my vibrations, so I could shake off the heavy energy I was carrying around with me. She told me to start saying my

I Choose Life

"Oms" every day to raise my vibrations. She told me to go to the ARE (Association of Research and Enlightenment) bookstore in Virginia Beach and buy a book called *11:11* by Solara (2) and that it would help me understand what was going on in the big picture about the earth and the universe.

She told me that she was my special "helper" and that I was "one of her people" and that she would actually be more help to me once she was on the "other side" because one above was like two on the ground. She told me that I could write to her when I had questions about what was going on with the circumstances in my life. She gave me her card so I would have her address. She told me that I had a very big mission in this lifetime, equivalent to a heavy class load in college, and that was why I needed to start working on raising my vibrations so I would be able to accomplish this work. She told my sister Anne that Marie's baby (Louise) would be fine after she was born. She said Louise would have some minor health issues that were indirectly caused by Marie's illness during her

Chapter One — How Did I Get Here?

pregnancy. Kelly told both of us that Louise was walking a short path in this lifetime and that she wasn't meant to live a long life. Kelly said Louise would have the experiences she needed in her short time here, and then it would be time for her to leave because her journey was done. When Louise was little, Anne was very nervous that she would die shortly but stopped being so nervous as Louise grew up to be pretty healthy.

I didn't know or understand half of the things Kelly told me, but something about the way she said them resonated deep inside me, and even though she seemed a little "out there" to me, I trusted her. I was a business major when I attended the College of William and Mary in Williamsburg, Virginia, and I never took any philosophy or religion classes while I was there. I had never heard of saying your "Oms," but something about it seemed imperative that I get started on this right away, so I started saying them while I was in the shower. In less than a minute, I could feel something good starting to happen in my body, and I decided that I was going to keep doing this every time I was in the shower. My "Oms" became my song in the shower, and I still say them when I am showering because it has become such a habit for me. I noticed when I got out of the shower and looked in the mirror that my eyes looked a little brighter, so that was another affirmation that this was something good for me.

Kelly told me over and over again that my son Drake would be fine and that he was a very big spiritual "test" for me. As the years went by, I really doubted that she knew what she was talking about but totally understood why she told me he was a big test for me. Dealing with the challenges he had from my sister's dysfunctional lifestyle and dying from cancer proved to bring a lot of growth for me. I was not always happy about how hard I had to work to find ways to deal with the challenges he created, but it pushed me to grow in ways I would have never grown if I didn't feel like my back was up against the wall for many years. I realize now that the big test was for me not to lose faith that he could turn out to be a well-adjusted,

Chapter One — How Did I Get Here?

functioning adult. There were many times when I felt like I wanted to "quit" and give up on him, but deep down I always knew that if I gave up, he would end up in jail or dead. I didn't like either one of those choices, so I kept working on improving and healing myself, even though I didn't always feel like it. I would also get impatient and angry about why Drake wasn't "all better" sooner, and yet all of those challenges have brought me to where I am today, and I really like the person I am today and where my life is going right now. I love being me now, and it felt terrible to be me when I started going to Al-Anon in 1992. The journey has definitely been difficult and challenging and yet totally worth it now that I am where I am right now, and my life has been totally transformed by making one small change at a time.

Kelly told me that she and some other "spirit guides" would be working with me in my dreams and that I would remember some of these dreams to help me deal with the challenges going on in my life. I was having a lot of sinus trouble at the time, and Kelly did some healing

I Choose Life

work on me with my eyes closed, and I felt and saw a flash of bright white light in my sinuses and could see it going through all of my sinus area like it was cleaning it out. My sinuses were in really good shape for months after she did that. Kelly also told me that I had two spirit guides that had been with me from the day of my birth and would be with me until the day I died. One of them was a Native-American chief, and Kelly told me that they are the best guides you can have. I also had a schoolteacher behind me explaining things to me so I would understand what was going on. She told me that I "knew" both of them from times I had meditated, and I had no idea what she was talking about.

After I was back in Cleveland, I had gone through a very rough week of dealing with issues with Drake, and it had seemed like every time I turned around, I was unexpectedly changing my plans to go to Drake's school or his counselor for something that had happened. One Friday morning, I was desperate to be able to exercise (which I had to miss the other days that week) for an hour and

Chapter One — How Did I Get Here?

have some time for myself. I had a minivan at the time, and I went in the back and got on my hands and knees and started praying that I could have a little bit of time for myself with no unexpected issues to deal with. When I was praying, I saw a photographic image of a woman's face that I had never seen before. I still remember what she looked like and the clothes she was wearing. I had no idea what had happened, and I finished praying and went to go exercise. The place where I exercised was in an office building with an elevator, and my exercise class was on the third floor. I got in the elevator, and when the doors opened, the woman whose face I had just seen was standing there in real life. I am sure I probably looked surprised when I saw her because this had never happened to me before.

I called Kelly to ask about this experience because I couldn't forget that woman's face and what had happened at the elevator. Kelly told me that this was a gift I had been born with and that I would eventually be using it to help other people. She told me that I would have to work to develop it and that it would develop very gradually as I worked on myself, and then I would be able to use it for the benefit of other people and their healing.

Mother Teresa

Part of my starting to read again involved reading books about Mother Teresa. I got a flyer from our church on Christian books, and there were two of them on Mother Teresa that were appealing to me, so I bought them and *loved* reading them. I did not grow up Catholic, but she just resonated with me, and I felt like I could read her stuff for hours and hours and hours because I liked the things she said and the stories she told.

It became very apparent to me that I needed to get some counseling to help me deal with Drake because it was like he had never been disciplined before, and some of his behavior was really unusual, and I had no idea what to do. Then I got the stomach flu and was lying on the couch during the day when my husband was at work, so I could watch my kids. Drake totally flipped out when

Chapter One — How Did I Get Here?

I was on the couch all day, and since he was four years old, it didn't matter what I said to him because the last "mommy" who had been on the couch all day had just died. That night I decided I was going to do whatever I needed to do to get myself really healthy so he wouldn't have to deal with my death for a while, and I also decided to find a child psychologist as soon as possible to help me with Drake. We worked with a child psychologist who helped me to learn a lot of effective parenting skills for dealing with a child whose mother had just died and also a child who had been physically abused. While none of my family would talk about Marie's hitting Drake, his counselor told me that there was really no question in his mind that Drake had been physically abused, and that was the source of some of the challenges with him.

As time went by, my mom and Anne started telling me horror stories of things that had happened to Drake when he was with Marie. Drake also started telling me about how he and Marie had spent the night in a church once and how they had slept in their car another night.

I Choose Life

Anne told me that Marie had called her one summer night and told her that she was at a party and had taken Drake with her, and they had found Drake floating face down in the swimming pool. Someone had done mouth to mouth on him, and he was revived. Marie was just going to go home until Anne told her that she needed to take Drake to an emergency room to be checked out since he had been unconscious when they pulled him out of the pool.

Then Drake told me that his dad, David, had gotten really mad one time when he was at Marie's apartment and had shaken Drake and then thrown him all the way up to the ceiling, and then Drake fell on the floor, and it hurt when he landed. Then Drake told me that one time David had gotten really mad at Marie and had pushed her off the balcony of their second-floor apartment. When I asked Anne about this, she told me Marie had been in the hospital a couple of days once with quite a few bruises, and Marie had told Anne and my mom that she had been in a car accident. Anne didn't know

Chapter One — How Did I Get Here?

anything about her being pushed off of a balcony but said that that would explain her injuries in the hospital better than a car accident did. Many years later, the wife of Drake's tennis coach called me after Drake was asked not to come back to his private boys' school and told me she felt so sorry for him since his father had killed his mother. When I asked her what she was talking about, she told me that one of the boys from Drake's school had told everyone at tennis that Drake's dad was in prison for killing his mother, and that was why Drake came to live with me. I had no idea what she was talking about when we were on the phone, but after we hung up, I realized that Drake must have told this story to kids at school, and they just assumed she died when she was pushed off the balcony. It was amazing that this story had been circulating behind the scenes for nine years at Drake's private school, and none of it was true at all. No one had ever asked me about it to find out if it was true, and yet I could always tell that there was something going on over there, but I couldn't figure out what it was. Rumors can be so harmful to everyone, especially when no one ever verifies if the story is true or not.

Discovering My Song

As I continued going to Al-Anon, I realized that my thinking about all the problems in my life was not doing me any good and was only making me feel worse. I decided that I wanted to find a way to change my thinking so I could start to feel better in spite of a lot of continuing daily challenges. Then at an Al-Anon meeting, I heard a woman who was an old-timer with many years in Al-Anon tell her story. She kept saying we need to "praise the Lord" whenever anything goes wrong because that is what the scriptures tell us to do. Initially I thought this was one of the craziest things I had ever heard. Then I reached a point where I was desperate enough that I thought to myself, *What do I have to lose if I try this?* I decided that if it worked then I would feel better, and if it didn't work then I wouldn't do it anymore. Amazingly it really did help me feel better when I did this, and I would

Chapter One — How Did I Get Here?

start thinking to myself, *Praise the Lord—another problem.* Then one day in the car, I decided to put on instrumental music and just think the words "praise the Lord" over and over again in my head as my own words to the music. After a twenty-five-minute drive to my daughter's school, I felt so good inside that I could hardly believe it, and I could hardly believe that it was relatively simple to have shifted to such a happier, lighter place than where I had been twenty-five minutes earlier. What I realized as I began to learn about primordial sound meditation was that "praise the Lord" had become a mantra for me, and I was meditating and didn't even know it.

"The song of rejoicing softens hard hearts, and draws forth from them tears, and invokes the Holy Spirit. God is music, God is life that nurtures every creature in its kind" (Newman, *Symphonia*). (3) Inventing my "Praise the Lord" song was softening and healing my heart without my even realizing it.

I learned later that focusing on a scripture verse is a form of centering prayer as well as a form of meditation.

My silent "singing" of my "Praise the Lord" song over and over again had taken me into my heart space. I felt better and better as I sang my song more and took my mind off of troubles and problems that would be there whether I spent time thinking about them or not.

Learning about Who I Was Born to Be

A friend of mine wanted to take an astrology class from a man who had a local radio show, and she asked me if I would take it with her. My mom and Anne had started taking astrology classes about nine months earlier in Virginia Beach, and they were using it to point out all my character defects and challenges in life. They were really bothering me with all the bad things they were telling me about myself, so I said yes, I would take this class—mostly out of self-defense and to see for myself if I was really as bad as they were telling me. This class proved to be life-changing for me because it helped me understand that I was being who I was created to be (per my astrology chart), which was different than my mom or Anne,

Chapter One — How Did I Get Here?

and that is why they didn't really understand me because they were very much alike. One night in that class, the man teaching it looked at my chart, and I could feel his concern about me. Then he looked up at me, and the look on his face was "Oh, my God, are you okay?" I know he didn't want to upset me, but I realized years later that he could see the trauma that happened in my childhood, and his response had really been one of compassion for me, and that was how it felt. Also without realizing it, he had affirmed the horror of some things that happened in my childhood that no one in my family of origin was willing to talk about openly.

My astrology teacher, Blake, told me that my chart was a "writer's dream" and wanted to know what I wrote. I told him that I didn't write anything, and he looked at me like he couldn't believe that was possible based on what he saw in my chart. He let it go, and in another class he asked me if I kept a journal. I told him that I had almost always had a journal, and he told me he knew that I was a writer and would probably end up writing popular books one day because that was the way my chart was set up. In another class, Blake asked me if I did artwork. I told him that I liked to make things, and that the only awards I won when I was growing up were for art: a watercolor picture I painted and a large twenty-five-inch octagon needlepoint picture I made that had several layers to it. I was trying to figure out why I hadn't taken art classes in school like both of my sisters had done, and I remembered my mother always telling me over and over again like a broken record that because I was so smart, I would be able to make a lot of money, and because of her goal for me, she had kept me away from art classes. She picked out my college major of business administration, and because I was obedient, I did what she told me. Then I remembered that when I was around five years old, I had watched the Miss America pageant with my mom, and then I got a notebook with paper in it and drew six or seven dress designs. I showed my designs to my mother, and instead of understanding what I had done, she made fun of my drawings and told me that the hands didn't look like real hands, and

Chapter One — How Did I Get Here?

the face didn't look like a real face, and I was crushed by her criticism of me. In a career-planning class I took after I graduated from college, I learned from an industrial psychologist that the things we do naturally as children that no one has asked us to do are where our real talents and skills are. I had also written five or six children's books when I was in high school that I would read to my brothers, and I drew the pictures to go with the stories. I liked the things I was learning about myself from my astrology chart, and it helped me to let go of some shame I had been carrying around from my childhood that I got from my mother not really understanding me and telling me I was "bad" frequently. Instead of realizing that I was basically of a different nature than she was, she had criticized me for many things about myself that were different than her. Yet, in the astrology class, I learned that many of the things she didn't like and criticized were things I was born with, and that was the way I was supposed to be. I was able to learn about my mother's chart and see very clearly how the two of us were different and had very different values in life. We

I Choose Life

also had totally different approaches to work and getting jobs done. I also knew, without a doubt, that my mother loved me, and Blake confirmed that when he very emphatically told me, "Your mother really *loved* you!" I told him I knew she loved me, and he said, "It shows in your chart and the way you just answered that." What I know now is that I am much more like my father and his family, so when he died, and I was only four years old, I lost the person who would have understood me when I was growing up and would have been able to nourish the parts of me that were like him. My father's family were very smart and accomplished – his older brother got his Ph.D. from MIT in Boston and his younger brother went to undergraduate school at Harvard and got his legal degree from Harvard Law School. I learned at a Junior League presentation that 50 percent of children who have a parent die when they are little end up becoming alcoholics and/or addicts. I learned in energy healing classes that losing a parent before reaching the age of seven leaves a hole (or a leak) in your second chakra (energy centers in the body). The second chakra is

Chapter One — How Did I Get Here?

where most addictions, except for nicotine and marijuana (these are fourth chakra problems), are caused. While I did not grow up to be an alcoholic (I don't even like most alcoholic beverages and haven't had any alcohol since 1994), I did marry one, and this made sense to me when I started learning more about how the events that happen to us in our lives affect the energy centers in our bodies, the issues we have around those energy centers, and the types of people we attract to us because of those energy issues.

I liked learning about astrology because it helped me understand that things happen to us in our lives usually during different astrological cycles that are going on. It is like the cycles are the switch "on" for certain events to start happening in our lives, and this is how things are supposed to unfold. It helped me to accept that events in my life were very normal for the transits that were going on when they happened in my chart.

After I had been taking astrology classes for a while, I felt much more comfortable talking about my astrology chart with my mom and Anne. It did not even bother me when they would be critical of me or my chart, because I had learned enough about my chart to know that I was exactly the way I was supposed to be.

One time when we were visiting my family in Virginia, my sister Anne had gotten a new job at the hospital and wanted me to come visit her at work in the NICU. Her new job was in a downtown hospital, and many of the babies in the NICU were African-American. When we walked in, and she took me over to see a little African-American boy in his Isolette, I felt very panicky, like I had to get out of there as fast as I could. Something about looking at that little baby was completely freaking me out. Anne looked at me and kept asking, "Are you okay?" I told her that I needed to get out of there, and she walked with me to the door of the NICU and thanked me for coming to visit her. I had no idea what had happened or why I was so uncomfortable seeing that little baby.

Drake continued to have many issues and challenges on an almost daily basis, and it was incredibly stressful for me to deal with. The stress of having to address daily

Chapter One — How Did I Get Here?

problems with Drake was compounded for me by my husband's attempts at getting and staying sober and being very difficult to deal with because of the way it affected his moods. I was using my "praise the Lord" mantra, listening to instrumental music as often as I could because this was really the only thing that was helping me to feel better and let go of some of the stress that seemed to be escalating the more I worked to calm myself down.

How Dick Got to AA

Then in May 1994, when I was at an Al-Anon meeting, I met a woman who told me that her husband would take my husband to an AA meeting if I could get him to agree to go. Drake had an incident at school that opened the door for me to approach my husband and tell him that I didn't think Drake was going to get much better unless Dick stopped drinking completely. I told him my friend's husband, who was a businessman, would take him to an AA meeting, and he agreed to go to AA with this man, James, who turned out to be his sponsor. They went to

I Choose Life

an AA meeting on a Friday night, and that Sunday afternoon my Mom called me and told me that she was in Washington, DC, at my grandfather's house because my grandfather was in the hospital. He had suffered an aneurism in his brain and collapsed in the shower, and they didn't expect him to live much longer. James had told me that he was going to take my husband to AA on Monday, Tuesday, and Thursday nights, and I panicked at the thought of Dick's not going to the meetings. Needing a way to get out of this, I told my mom, "He can't die until Thursday or Friday, so Dick can go to more AA meetings." My mother got really mad and then said to me, "Who do you think you are that you can have control over life and death?" I told her that I knew my grandfather was going to end up dying; I just needed him to wait until Thursday or Friday. Well, my mom called me on Thursday morning and told me, "Grandaddy waited for you; he just died." This was my first concrete "God moment" that really strengthened my faith in a Power greater than myself helping me with my life. I also know

Chapter One — How Did I Get Here?

now that my grandfather adored me; he always told me, "You'll always be number one with me, doll" every time I saw him, and I realized many years later that that had been his way of telling me I was his favorite without upsetting my sisters and brothers. It was a huge loss for me because, in many ways, my grandfather had been my father since my dad died when I was only four years old.

After the funeral, I was sitting on the back porch of my grandfather's house eating lunch with my mother, and she started talking about her mother, who had died when I was nine years old. My mom told me that her mother would just sit in her bedroom and drink and not come out of her room for hours and hours. When my mother told me this, I looked at her and said, "Your mother was an alcoholic." I did not expect my mother's reaction at all because she got really mad and said to me, "No, she wasn't an alcoholic; she just liked to drink." I did not argue with my mom about this, but it actually felt like a gift from God to find out how I had married an alcoholic when my mother didn't drink very much

I Choose Life

at all. Then I remembered that my mother had a framed copy of the "Serenity Prayer" on her dresser, and she told me that a friend of my grandfather had given it to her a long time ago and told her that it was a very special prayer that would help her. My mother kept that framed "Serenity Prayer" on her dresser for all of my life, and then I realized one day that my grandfather must have also gone to Al-Anon because of my grandmother, and that was how he knew this woman who had tried to help my mom by giving her a copy of that prayer. The sad thing to me is that even though my mother always had the "Serenity Prayer" on her dresser, she never found her way to Al-Anon or even understood at all why it was a special prayer that would help her. Then it dawned on me that going to Al-Anon was probably one of the reasons that it seemed like my grandfather knew everyone when I was little, and we would go to the grocery store or drug store to run errands—many of those people were probably some of his Al-Anon friends.

Chapter One — How Did I Get Here?

My grandfather died at the age of ninety, and his only health problems were false teeth, hearing aids, and special shoes to keep his balance. He still drove a car and lived in his own house with no problems. There were a lot of people at his funeral, and I asked my grandmother one day how many people had been there; she told me that about 275 people had signed the guest book, and I was totally impressed that my grandfather had that many people at his funeral, and he was ninety years old. I decided that I wanted to age and grow old the way that my grandfather had because I liked that he was basically very strong and healthy until the last four days of his life.

After my grandfather died, and I was spending a week in Hatteras, North Carolina, with my mom, Anne and her kids, my husband and kids, my grandmother, Billy, Joe, and my Uncle Stuart, I was talking to Joe about my grandfather and how neatly dressed he always was. Joe made the comment that he had never seen my grandfather in just a t-shirt or really casual clothes of any kind. Then Joe was joking around a little bit and said that it was almost like every day was "church" day because he was always so nicely dressed. This idea of my grandfather always being nicely dressed stayed with me for some reason, and I started thinking that I only dressed that nicely when I had something "important" to go to like a social function or a meeting of some kind. Then when I was walking one day, it dawned on me that every day had been important to my grandfather, and that was why he was always dressed nicely. So I decided that I wanted to dress like every day was important for me as well.

This was a huge step for me to allow myself to have that many nice outfits because in my family growing up, my mom would have considered that extremely selfish and would not have agreed at all. Yet the combination of Marie's death and now my grandfather's death made it more important than ever for me to feel like I was really living each day to its fullest since none of us really knows when our final breath will come. This also motivated me to buy only things that I really liked and not to settle for things that would make do because life is short, and I

Chapter One — How Did I Get Here?

didn't want to keep waiting for "someday" to get here for me to get some of the things that I really liked. This ended up having a really big impact on me in the long run—much more than I would have ever expected or guessed when I got the idea to make this change. I immediately started to feel better when I was wearing nice outfits every day, and other people treated me better when I had on nicer clothes. As time went by, I got really good at knowing what would work on my body and what I would and wouldn't wear. It started to be really fun for me to put together nice clothes and outfits and to make them look pretty by either the color combinations or adding some jewelry. Then I had people coming up to me and telling me that they felt better after seeing me because I looked so "pretty" to them. My dentist commented to me once that I was "just like a breath of fresh air" walking into his office in such a pretty outfit. So part of the ripple effect of my making this change was that my "nice" appearance affected other people around me in a good way. Since I grew up at the beach, I am basically a pretty casual person, and I have found a lot of ways to be completely comfortable and still look "nice" without having to put a lot of time and effort into getting dressed in the morning.

The combination of Dick's new sobriety, my grandfather's death, and Drake's continuing problems was extremely stressful for me. In addition to going to an aerobics class two times a week, I started walking in my neighborhood every day, especially when my husband was going through "dry drunk" episodes. There were so many problems and so much confusion going on that I didn't really know what to pray about or pray for, so I used my "praise the Lord" mantra as I walked in my neighborhood to calm myself down from the major chaos in my house at that time.

I had never learned about meditation and had no idea of how much time is a good amount of time to meditate during a day. I also did not understand at all about the importance of being grounded and alternating between meditation and daily activities. I learned about

Chapter One — How Did I Get Here?

these things many years later when I went to the Chopra Center for the first time. It really helped me to learn about the basics of meditation so I could understand what had happened to me in September 1995, and the importance of maintaining balance between meditation and activity every day.

Chapter Two — The Memories I Didn't Know I Had

I remember being in the back seat of my husband's car in September 1995. I had just gotten out of the hospital and didn't really remember everything that had happened to me, but I remembered about two-thirds of it. I had three or four prescriptions that I had to take when I got home, and my husband was telling me that I had had a nervous breakdown and needed to get counseling for sexual abuse because the social worker at

I Choose Life

the hospital was positive that I had been sexually abused as a child. I had no idea what he was talking about and had never even dreamed or been aware at all that I had been sexually abused when I was growing up.

What I know now is that I had repressed memories and incidents that I had disassociated from because they had been so traumatic. I remembered parts of what had happened and also while I was in the hospital, and I have had five different counselors tell me that no one ever remembers anything after a nervous breakdown, and they don't understand what happened to me that triggered my memories to come up. Three of these counselors told me that they didn't know what had happened to me, but it wasn't really a classic nervous breakdown because I remembered so much of what happened. What I figured out on my own was that by using my "praise the Lord" mantra more and more, I was meditating way too much for a beginner, and I opened up my kundalini way too fast and had basically blown out my circuits by doing this. I blew

Chapter Two — The Memories I Didn't Know I Had

out my kundalini, and the doctors had no awareness or diagnosis for this. I had two different psychiatrists, and my last one told me after he had seen me for six years that there was absolutely nothing wrong with me, that I was healthier than he was, and he had absolutely no idea what had happened to me when I had experienced a psychotic break with reality in 1995, mixing up the memories from my childhood trauma with what was going on around me in physical reality.

Healing My Heart

After I got home, I kept seeing an image in my head of my mom sitting in a rocking chair in my grandfather's living room; she was holding my heart up to her heart as she rocked slowly and gently in the rocking chair and looking out the front window at me going around and gathering up the thousand pieces of me that had been "torn" apart during my life. I had the energy to look and find the pieces while my mom sat there holding my heart up to hers. Looking back on this, it was as if I had opened a box with a thousand puzzle pieces in it, and I had no picture to guide me of what the puzzle was supposed to look like. I had to figure out how the pieces fit together and what the picture was supposed to look like all on my own.

The first time I talked to my mom on the telephone after I got out of the hospital, I told her that the social worker there told me they were sure that I was sexually abused when I was growing up. My mom gasped and then in a horrified voice said, "You remembered that? Dr. Rosen [her psychiatrist] told me you would never remember that!" Then I asked her what she was talking about, and she changed the subject and would never talk about it again, although later in that same conversation, she told me that my brother Joe had asked her when he was in high school if his Dad had ever "messed" with Marie. My mom asked him why he wanted to know, and he told her that he was wondering because Marie was "so screwed up." This was all the information I ever got from my mom, and since Marie was dead and Anne was four years younger than I was, there was no one else to really

Chapter Two — The Memories I Didn't Know I Had

confirm anything about what had happened. When I was talking to a counselor about my mom's initial response and then her refusal to ever talk about it again, the counselor told me that it was because my mother had never forgiven herself, and because of that she couldn't talk about it with me. The counselor told me that this was denial, and it was how my mom was coping with what happened and her guilt about the incidents and that I would probably never be able to get her to talk about it unless she managed to forgive herself for what had happened.

If I had known what I was going to remember as a result of my "Praise the Lord" song, I probably would have stopped singing this song forever because of the incredible pain that was there with the memories. Remembering my traumas and the emotions that went with them was the worst pain I have ever felt in my life and made me feel like I understood people who wanted to kill themselves because, if I had a different personality, I would have probably chosen that option. After processing the pain from these traumas, I completely understand why

I Choose Life

some people choose suicide as their best option to put an end to the pain inside of them. Deep down inside, I have always wanted to live and have had a strong feeling that my life would get better as I got older.

After I was home for a couple of weeks, I did remember some pieces of things from my childhood that were sort of strange, but I couldn't remember the whole event of what had happened around those pieces. I had heard someone at my church talk about being hypnotized to remember some childhood trauma, so I got the name of this therapist and made an appointment to meet with her. The first piece I could remember on my own was of being naked on all fours on my mother and stepfather's bed in the house we lived in in Jacksonville, Florida. When I was hypnotized, I remembered that my nine-month-pregnant mother had called me into her room to take a shower and told me to take all of my clothes off. Then my stepfather came behind me, closed the bedroom door, and then yelled at my mother to "get her on the bed," and she told me to get on all fours on the bed. Then

Chapter Two — The Memories I Didn't Know I Had

my naked stepfather came up behind me and raped me. I was screaming and yelling because it had hurt, and my mother had told me to do this. That was my initial memory from this trauma in 1995. It has taken me eighteen years of daily forgiveness work, meditation, yoga, dream work, and energy work to remember all of the pieces of this trauma. All the pieces did not come back at once, and I realize now after I remembered the last two pieces that it was because of the depth of the initial injury to my heart at the apparent betrayal by my mom. At the time I was horrified when people were telling me that they wanted to read my book about these things because it would make my mom look bad, and I knew she loved me. With every ounce of my being, I knew beyond a shadow of a doubt that my mother loved me unconditionally and completely. It was because I had not remembered the final two pieces of this incident that I kept putting off writing this book, even though I have been writing and working on things that are a part of this book for at least ten years and maybe a little longer.

I Choose Life

As I worked with this initial piece that I had been able to retrieve under hypnosis, I remembered that after that had happened, I wanted my mom to give me a hug because she had always done that to help me feel better when I had been upset or hurt before this. Yet my stepfather was screaming at my mom and kept saying to her, "Don't you dare help that little bi-ch; she doesn't deserve it." My mother was five feet tall and nine months pregnant, and my stepfather was six-one and built like a linebacker, so he was physically very, very intimidating, and he was raging mad. There was no way my mother would have ever attempted to physically fight with him or go against him, especially since she was nine months pregnant. I lay on the floor beside my mother's bed for hours, screaming and crying for her to help me and give me a hug because my dad was dead, and I needed my mother more than I had ever needed her in my life, and this man was forbidding her to help me. I don't know how long I was there on the floor sobbing, but I know it was a very long time because I couldn't believe that my mother

Chapter Two — The Memories I Didn't Know I Had

was right there and not helping me when I needed her the most with every ounce of my being. I could feel my mother's heart breaking because she wanted to help me, but my stepfather would not let her. At some point I got up and went to my own bed, and I remember that the next morning, when it was time for school, my mom came in my room and whispered in my ear for me to pretend that I was sick because she had called the school and told them I was sick and not coming in that day.

After my sister went to school, and my stepfather had gone to work, my mom came in my room and told me she was so sorry this had happened to me. She scooped me up, gave me a hug, and took me to sit in her rocking chair with me on her lap. It didn't matter that she was nine months pregnant; she just held me on her lap and rocked very slowly and gently in her rocking chair. We were in that chair for hours until my mom very gently told me that we needed to get up because my sister would be home soon, and we needed to get dressed. This could not erase the effects of what had happened completely, but it did make me feel better and let me know that my mother did love me. I know now that she was also victimized by witnessing me go through this, and her suffering was worse than mine because she had to witness what happened to me and was totally powerless to prevent it or help me in any way.

Dealing with Resentment

I had a huge amount of resentment toward my mom and my stepfather after I remembered this trauma, and that is putting it mildly. When I was quiet with myself, I felt like my entire being was consumed with this resentment toward both of them. There is a line in one of the Al-Anon pieces of literature that says, "Forgiveness and making amends for our own mistakes are essential tasks in the process of recovering and beginning to live in the present." I wanted to start working on forgiveness, so I could be living in the present and not consumed by the anger and resentment inside of me. I was also really mad at God for letting these things happen to me. Then

Chapter Two — The Memories I Didn't Know I Had

at an Al-Anon meeting, someone did a program based on the Big Book from AA, and they talked about how if you prayed for someone's health, happiness, and prosperity for at least twenty-one days, you would begin to experience a change of heart toward the person you had resentment for. So I went home and started praying for the health, happiness, and prosperity of my mom and my stepfather. I felt like I was almost going to die to pray this for my stepfather, and yet I knew I wanted to get better, so I kept doing this so I could be rid of the "ickiness" of this resentful feeling inside my being. Twenty-one days of this prayer did not even touch the resentment because it was so big inside of me. Somehow I intuitively knew that I had to keep praying this prayer to get rid of this resentment, so I kept praying for their health, happiness, and prosperity when I got up in the morning and before I went to sleep at night. At some point I stopped worrying about how long I had been praying this prayer and just did it as part of my daily routine and figured I would "know" when it was better.

I Choose Life

I can remember driving on Chagrin Boulevard in Beachwood, Ohio, with my kids one afternoon and all of a sudden realizing "it" was gone. The bitterness and resentment I had carried for many years was gone, and it felt like a miracle had happened. This incredible resentment was just gone, and I didn't wish that my stepfather would die anymore. This was a little over two and a half years after I had started praying this prayer. That was how deep this injury had been within me. I tell people this in Al-Anon, so they will know that some emotional injuries take much longer than twenty-one days to heal and release and to stick with it, and they will eventually be able to feel better and heal the injury.

My stepfather was also physically abusive of us when we were growing up. He would pull off his belt to spank us when we did something wrong. This had the effect of totally immobilizing me because the things he would get upset about were irrational and not always predictable. I never knew what would set him off at random times, and I became an expert at being able to detect the subtle

Chapter Two — The Memories I Didn't Know I Had

changes that would take place in his behavior right before he was going to explode. I got really, really good at being able to feel it coming. Because I had to use this skill to literally keep myself alive, and I used it all the time, it eventually gave me a very strong knowing that I can survive anything no matter what circumstances I am in.

My stepfather's physical abuse of me came to an end when I was sixteen. I remember being on my way to go babysit the little boys next door to us, and one of my siblings needed the glue. We would usually only own one container of glue for the five of us to share. My mom asked me if I knew where the glue was, and I told her I didn't and kept walking toward the front door. The next thing I knew was my stepfather had his belt off, swinging it around in the air with a crazy look on his face, and he started screaming at me for not helping to look for the glue. Something snapped inside of me, and I decided he was not going to hit me with his belt over not knowing where a bottle of glue was. I believe in the powers of adrenalin because I am five-three, and he was

I Choose Life

a sturdy six-one, and I went over to him, pushed his chest, and backed him up to a wall then told him that if he hit me, he was going to be sorry. The adrenalin was flowing when I pushed him like he was nothing, and there was a split second when I instantly knew that I could really hurt this man if I wanted to because of how mad I was. Also in that instant, my stepfather seemed to realize and acknowledge that I could really hurt him if I wanted to. I was suddenly in control, and I wanted him to try to hit me so I could have an excuse to really hurt him, but my stepfather backed off and let me leave to go next door.

When I got next door, the woman gave me a hug and asked me if I was okay. I told her I was because I had learned a long time ago not to tell the truth about what was happening in my house—especially not to tell anything about my stepfather to anyone. Looking back on this, I am sure the woman next door to us knew there was abuse going on and was afraid to get involved or do anything about it.

Chapter Two — The Memories I Didn't Know I Had

My stepfather never attempted to hit me after that incident because we both knew that I could hurt him if I wanted to because of what had happened. Even though he stopped hitting me, I was always aware of where he was in the house and whether he was getting ready to explode or not. I walked on eggshells around him and worked as hard as I could to not do anything that would set him off, and I was trying to be perfect all the time. What I didn't realize when I did this is that I didn't do much of anything else besides my schoolwork because my only priority was to be safe and stay alive at all costs. I was terrified of giving my stepfather a legitimate excuse for beating me up, so I never explored who I was as an adolescent because I was literally trying to stay alive. I had no idea of what I was good at doing or had a passion for doing.

I like a quote from Mother Teresa: "God Himself cannot fill what is full. That's why we need forgiveness to become empty and God fills us with Himself." (4)As I emptied myself of my many resentments, God began to fill me up with Himself and His love for me, and this allowed me to start to really love myself for who I was born to be. Through this process I became more and more alive than I had ever been before. I felt more vital and alert than I had been in my whole life. I had a lot of injuries or "holes" to let God's light shine out of me to others. The cracked vessel allows more light to shine out than any whole and complete vessel, and I came to see that my injuries that had healed within me gave me the ability to send out a lot of light from my being. Then I would look at the mirror sometimes and think, *Who is that?* because my physical appearance had changed again after I had forgiven more things and learned to love myself more. This happened almost a half a dozen times that I remember because all of sudden I wouldn't recognize myself in the mirror. Forgiveness was allowing me to not feel so much pain inside of myself like I had when I started coming to Al-Anon.

The good thing is that after twenty-one years of recovery work, I can catch myself very quickly if I start to go back into "stinking thinking" or other nonproductive

Chapter Two — The Memories I Didn't Know I Had

behaviors. I have a total understanding of what tools work for me when I am faced with a challenge or difficult situation, and I wouldn't have learned these tools or learned how to do this for myself if I had not had so many emotional injuries to work on. Then I found a quote—"Other people can rape and damage my body. Only I can damage my soul"—from a female American-Indian elder, and I realized that parts of my soul might have been damaged or gone missing in my childhood, but the core of my soul was what was giving me the energy and motivation to heal and get better. This was another big "God moment" for me.

More Pieces to the First Memory

What I remembered three months ago was that even though my stepfather was yelling at my mom the entire time I was on the floor crying for her to help me, my mom had very slowly but surely scooted herself over to the edge of her bed and very, very quietly dropped her right arm and hand down on the floor to touch my head, and I was able to hug her arm and start to feel better. I felt ecstatic when I remembered this piece because it helped me to know that my mom did really love me and that she had done what she could to try to help me in spite of being in physical danger herself. When I remembered that she had tried to help me, I also knew something I had never been aware of before, and that was when I was hurt and crying on the floor with no one to help me, it was when I had wanted to die for the first time. Since my father had died and wasn't there, and my mother wasn't able to help me, I wished I was dead because there was no point in living if no one loved me. When I learned about dream work from a man, Robert Moss, who was knowledgeable about shamanic and Native-American dream work, I found out that traumatic incidents like this cause us to lose parts of our souls (vital life forces) that can't stand to be there anymore because of what trauma or injury had happened. I have worked with many counselors and energy healers about how a part of me has never been the same since this incident, even

Chapter Two — The Memories I Didn't Know I Had

when I was remembering the pieces after I got out of the hospital. Well, when I remembered this about my mom's arm and hand being there for me, I knew that I had just retrieved a very big piece of my soul that had been missing since I was nine years old, when this originally happened to me.

Then about a month ago, during a long meditation I was doing, I remembered a much bigger piece of this trauma. I remembered that when I had initially walked into my mom's bedroom, my stepfather was already completely naked and was physically aroused. He was standing beside my mother with a knife in his hand fairly close to her neck, and my mother was quietly crying with tears streaming down her cheeks. My stepfather told my mother that she had to do everything he said or he was going to slit her throat and then kill her little "bi-ch," too, and my mother just shook her head like "Okay, I will do what you say." Then my stepfather looked at me and told me that he was going to kill me if I told anyone about this. When I saw the knife at my mother's throat, and my stepfather told me that he would kill me if I told anyone, I wanted to die immediately because it would be impossible for me not to tell anyone that my stepfather had a knife to my mother's throat and was threatening to kill her right in front of me. This idea seemed too much for me to bear, and I would have rather been dead than witness him kill my mother in front of me. My mother was crying the entire time my stepfather raped me and when I was lying on the floor next to their bed crying for her to help me. What I remembered was that in addition to my stepfather's yelling at her not to help me the whole time was that he still had a knife close to my mom's throat after they got in bed and was threatening to still hurt her if she helped me at all. After I remembered the knife, I cried and cried at the pain and agony and heartbreak I can only imagine my mother lived through that night, and I am telling you that my mother was never the same again after that trauma. I figured out after I remembered this that my mother also lost a part of her soul that night

Chapter Two — The Memories I Didn't Know I Had

when she had to watch me be hurt and suffer and then was prevented from helping me. In many ways it was as if my mother died that night because she was really broken and different for the rest of her life. This last part of me I retrieved was the part that was born to be a writer and has been missing since I was nine years old. This was why I never understood why the astrologers got so excited about my chart as the "writer's d ream chart." The part of me that was born to do this had been gone since I was nine. When working to complete the paperwork to join the Daughters of the American Revolution (DAR), I learned that one of my father's relatives wrote three books on geneology. So now I understand where the writing ability came from in my family.

Then when I was thinking about how much work and energy it has taken me to retrieve the last piece of this memory, I thought of the song "The First Cut Is the Deepest," and my "first cut" had ripped the middle out of my soul and soul purpose in this lifetime. I realized that my stepfather was a terrorist in the truest sense of the word, and it was a miracle that we survived that night. Then I remembered something a nun, Sister Sarah, had told me shortly after I got out of the hospital—that she was seeing terror in my eyes, complete and full-blown terror. I had no idea at the time what Sister Sarah was talking about, even though my gut knew she was correct in what she was telling me. My mother was pregnant with my brother Billy when this happened. Billy has struggled back and forth many years to be sober. I asked an energy counselor if Billy going through this trauma in utero would make him an alcoholic, and the counselor got tears in his eyes, thought about it for a minute, and sadly shook his head yes and said there was really no way for him or my mother to have avoided this.

After I remembered and processed the final piece of this big trauma, I knew deep down inside of me that it was time for me to tell my story, stop keeping secrets, and use my healing as a way to offer encouragement and hope to other sexual abuse survivors who have not been allowed to tell their secrets to the world. Right after I

Chapter Two — The Memories I Didn't Know I Had

made this decision, there were two things on Facebook that I felt were affirmations from the universe to me. The first one was, "When you stand and share your story in an empowering way, your story will heal you and your story will heal somebody else" by Iyanla Vanzant. (5) The other one was, "You are contributing a huge piece of healing here by your willingness to tell the truth over and over again no matter how painful" by Marissa Gottlieb Sarles. (6) Then I heard a song on the radio when I got in my car, "It's Time," by Imagine Dragons and I was absolutely certain that it was "time" for me to write my book and share my story with the world.

More Memories

So once this initial memory had come back to me after I got out of the hospital, I started remembering other things that happened. I remembered a dead African-American baby boy hanging from a hangman's noose. My stepfather's family owned a 550-acre tobacco farm north of Myrtle Beach in South Carolina, and when you were there in the house or one of the barns, you were truly in the middle of nowhere, and there was no one who would ever know what was happening there unless you called someone on the phone or had a way to send signals with a flashlight. My stepfather and two of his brothers were involved with the Ku Klux Klan, and one night my stepfather made my mother take me into the barn with them. There were about seven or eight of them in a circle, wearing the white outfits of the Ku Klux Klan. Then a man stepped into the center and took a live, newborn African-American baby and put a hangman's noose around the baby's neck. He brought the baby about three feet away from my face and screamed at me that he was going to kill this little bas-ard, and if I told anyone what he did, he would kill me too. Then he pulled the noose really tight and broke that baby's neck, and then the rest of them had sticks they used to beat it into a bloody mess. Even with his Ku Klux Klan outfit on, I knew that the voice talking to me was my stepfather, and I recognized his hands. There is absolutely no doubt in my mind that he is the one who killed that newborn baby. I

Chapter Two — The Memories I Didn't Know I Had

told this story to Anne, and her first reaction was that the baby was probably his, and he needed to get rid of it so no one would know he had been sleeping with one of the migrant workers on the farm. Then I remembered that this baby was long and skinny, just like Joe had been when he came home from the hospital, and this baby probably was my stepfather's illegitimate son. Then Anne looked at me and said that that was probably why I had freaked out when I came to visit her in the NICU. I didn't know what she was talking about, and I asked her, "What do you mean?" Anne said that she had worked in the NICU a long time, and she had never had anyone else have the reaction that I did when I saw the African-American baby boy in an Isolette, and this incident would explain why I had such a strong emotional reaction that no one else ever had.

There were a lot of migrant African-American workers on the farm, and the baby could have been born to any of the women. They treated these migrant workers like they were animals, and I was always bothered by this because, as far as I was concerned, they were people, too, and I liked talking to some of them and didn't like seeing them treated like animals. I felt sorry for whoever was the mother of this baby and had her newborn ripped away from her and then killed. Then I kept thinking to myself, *What kind of a person kills his own child, his own flesh and blood?* I did not understand how he could have done this. Joe had told me that his grandfather (my stepfather's dad) had gotten the police to come after the Ku Klux Klan and get them away from the farm. Several years later, Joe told me that my stepfather's brother, Derek, was being sued by his ex-wife for sexual abuse of his daughter.

This memory of the dead baby was really terrifying for me because of the death threat attached to it if I ever told anyone what had happened. Now that I remembered, I couldn't not tell someone what had happened to me, and yet the idea of speaking it out loud was terrifying me because it seemed like once I told this to another person, it would be out there in the universe, and on some level my stepfather would know and follow through on

Chapter Two — The Memories I Didn't Know I Had

his threat to kill me if I ever told anyone. I finally got the courage to tell this to a counselor, who told me it was a total and complete miracle that I was able to remember this since it was a death threat that had been kept buried and repressed all of these years. She kept asking me how I had managed to retrieve this memory because she saw a lot of people who knew they had repressed memories, and she did not know how to help them retrieve them so they could heal. Then she looked at me and said, "You did not have a breakdown; you had a huge breakthrough because now that you remember this, you will be able to heal it." Now I know that it was my meditation practice of saying my "Oms" in the shower and my "praise the Lord" mantra that brought this memory and the others into my awareness instead of keeping them buried deep inside of me. I told an Al-Anon friend of mine about how afraid I had been to tell this out loud, and she told me that she had a friend who was dying of cancer who had been sexually abused by her brother, and he had told her that if she ever told anyone, she would die, and she was joking and telling me that at least my stepfather hadn't told me that I was going to die if I ever told anyone the truth.

I had gotten into a habit of walking outside before my breakdown and wanted to start walking again after I was home from the hospital, but I was terrified to leave my house and walk outside after I told this memory to someone because now it was out there in the universe, and I was terrified that my stepfather would follow through on his threat to kill me. It took several weeks before I could work up my courage to go outside and walk, and the first few times I went outside, I only walked for about fifteen minutes because then I was afraid again. I was gradually able to start walking for thirty minutes again, but it was a really big hurdle for me to get over to go back outside again after I told about this memory. Even though Anne and Joe both told me things that in my mind affirmed that these things really happened, now, many years later, my brother Joe is denying that any of it is true. It dawned on me that this is why so many sexual abuse victims never tell their stories because other people in their families put

Chapter Two — The Memories I Didn't Know I Had

so much pressure on them to not tell the family "secrets." In Al-Anon, we talk a lot about how we are only as sick as our secrets. This is one secret that no one wants to talk about—even at Al-Anon, where there are pretty open-minded people at the meetings.

Trying to Stay Alive

The next memory came back to me like I was watching a movie of me when I was ten years old. This one occurred in a house we lived in that was in Patuxent River, Maryland. We had a four-bedroom ranch house; the fourth bedroom was behind the garage that had been converted into a family room. It was a bedroom with a small bathroom behind the family room. I was given this as my bedroom since I was the oldest, but I didn't like being in this room because it felt very far away from the other three bedrooms, and it scared me to be in there. There was a door in my room that went outside, which also made me feel vulnerable that someone could just walk into my room from outside.

I Choose Life

The "movie" of my memory that I saw was of me asleep in my bed, and my stepfather came into my room in his underwear, and he was physically aroused. I wasn't really sure why he was there, but I knew it was not good, so I rolled off the side of my bed that was the farthest away from the bedroom door, and he came closer to my bed. When he couldn't find me, he yelled, "Where did you go, you little bi-ch?" I crawled over to the bathroom, slammed the door shut as fast as I could, and then locked the door. Then he ran over to the bathroom door and started banging on it, yelling that the door wouldn't keep him away from me and that he was going to break it down. I yelled back at him that I was going to climb out the bathroom window and go outside, and he wouldn't be able to get me. Then he ran and went out the door to the backyard and over to where the bathroom window was, and I ran out of the bathroom and slammed the back door shut and locked it so he wasn't able to get back into my room.

A few days later, I heard him walking down the hall toward my room. He was big and heavy and walked very

Chapter Two — The Memories I Didn't Know I Had

heavily on his feet so that the whole floor of the house shook when he walked, and I knew he was coming because of the way the floor was shaking. I got out of bed and stayed on the floor by the bed, waiting to see what he would do. He walked all the way into the room and up to the bed, so I quickly and very quietly went behind him and out the bedroom door, and then I ran as fast as I could to my sister's room down the hall and slid into about a six-inch space between the dresser and the wall, praying that he wouldn't find me and waiting to hear him walk back to his bedroom. I heard him coming, but he stopped and came into my sister's room. My heart was racing, and I was terrified he would find me. He came in and looked around the room several times. He was probably there for about five minutes, but it felt like five hours to me while I was waiting to see if he would find me. Then I heard him leave and walk back to his own bedroom. I waited a few more minutes to make sure he didn't come back and that I would be okay, and then I crawled into the double bed with my sisters and went to sleep.

I Choose Life

I don't know how much time went by, but he came back and found me sound asleep in bed with my sisters, and then he grabbed me by the back of my neck, like they grab animals on the farm, and started yelling at me that I was such a little bi-ch, and he was going to teach me a lesson for thinking I could get away from him. Then he was saying that this was what he did to little bi-ches that tried to get away from him. He turned on the shower connected to my sister's bedroom and started shoving my head under the water and holding it there. I couldn't breathe; I was choking, and then I felt like I was drowning, and I thought he was going to kill me. Then I saw an army of a thousand angels in front of me, and they pushed me back and told me to kick him in the groin as hard as I could. I did, and he screamed really loudly and then threw me down to the ground extremely hard because now he was even madder than he had been before, and he left me there on the floor by the shower. When I fell on the ground, I hit my head on the edge of the shower and was knocked out. I was still unconscious

Chapter Two — The Memories I Didn't Know I Had

but could hear what was going on around me like it was a dream, and I heard my mom and stepfather talking beside me in the bathroom. My stepfather was telling her that he couldn't wake me up and that he thought I was dead. My stepfather told my mom he was going to take my clothes off and push me in the shower, and then he would tell the police that I had fallen in the shower. He pulled my nightgown off and shoved me all the way into the shower. He didn't realize that I still had my underwear on and that there was a small drip of water coming from the showerhead. I woke up at some point the next day with single drops of water that kept dripping on the middle of my forehead, and I was in the shower in only my underwear. I had no idea of why I was in the shower with my underwear on or how I had gotten there. I got up out of the shower, got dressed, and walked into the kitchen in front of my stepfather, feeling very proud of myself and thinking, *I'm alive. You didn't kill me. I won, and you lost!* I knew I had beaten this man and kept him from having total power over me and from being able to rape me again. My stepfather looked at me like he was seeing a ghost.

The first counselor I worked on with this told me that I had completely disassociated from this memory, and that was why I felt like I was watching a movie instead of actually having the memory inside of me. Then another counselor told me that when I had walked into the kitchen with the "I'm alive" attitude, my response was really healthy because in my own way I was telling my stepfather, "F-ck you!" and that was a really healthy response for me to have. I told this memory to Anne and was talking to her about how I wondered how my stepfather had gotten back in the house after I had locked him outside in only his underwear. She didn't even bat an eye and told me that my mom had let him in. I asked her why Mom would have done that and not questioned him about only being in his underwear, and we figured out that my mom was seven or eight months pregnant with my brother Joe, and, in her mind, she needed to stay married to him so she could feed us.

Chapter Two — The Memories I Didn't Know I Had

Anne turned to me and said that this incident was probably how I had gotten my deviated septum, and I knew deep inside of me that she was right. I had to do a lot of emotional work and forgiveness work toward my mother for letting him act like I had fallen in the shower, and when I was talking to Anne about it, she said my mom was probably trying to think of how to stay out of jail because she thought I was dead. Even though that logically made sense to me, it was a really difficult thing for me to deal with emotionally and to be able to let go completely of the pain from this.

One day I remembered the look of extreme concern on my astrology teacher Blake's face and his looking at me like something horrific had happened to me, and I realized that this and the other events must have been what he saw in my astrology chart that night. I will never forget how strongly I could feel his energy coming toward me in a sincere "are you okay?" kind of way. This was another event that had made me feel like I wanted to die instead of continuing to live with this terrorist in my house. It seemed like there was no point in continuing to live if my own mother had been aware of the attempted cover-up of what had happened to me. Anne worked with energy healers when she was older, and she told me that she could not energetically go back to that house and that two or three healers had tried to get her back into that house to figure out what happened and help her heal from whatever it was. What I know now is that it is worse to be the observer seeing someone almost killed than to be the victim of that abuse. Anne was only six years old when this happened to me, and she was in the bedroom that had its own bathroom, where my stepfather almost drowned me, and had most likely witnessed the whole thing. It is sad but not surprising to me that Anne was not able to feel safe or strong enough to go back in that house and remember what had happened that was an energy block for her.

The Worst of the Traumas

The last traumatic event I remembered happened one Saturday morning when my mother had gone to the

Chapter Two — The Memories I Didn't Know I Had

grocery store and left all of the kids at home with my stepfather. My stepfather walked into the family room, pulled out a switchblade knife, and told me to get into his car with him because he was taking me on an errand with him. At first I told him I wasn't going to get in the car, but then he started waving his knife around and yelling at me, "You are a little bi-ch. Get in the car or I am going to kill you right now." Then he came closer to me with the knife pointed right at me, and it was very clear to me that he meant what he said. I swallowed very hard, choked back tears, and got into his orange Volkswagen Beetle. I knew better than to say anything because that would just set him off again. I had no idea where we were going, and in my mind I was terrified that he was taking me somewhere to kill me just like he had killed that newborn baby. I closed my eyes and pretended that I was asleep because I didn't want him to try to talk to me. It was very rare for him to say anything nice to me, and I didn't want to hear any more ugly words out of his mouth. I don't remember the rest of the ride, and I think I fell asleep during part

I Choose Life

of the trip. We ended up on the farm in South Carolina, an eight-hour drive from our house in Maryland. Shortly after we got there, my stepfather talked to his family, and then he got his brother to come with him, and my stepfather pulled out his knife and ordered me to go out to the barn that was the closest to the house. After we were up in the loft, my stepfather pulled out a knife and started yelling at me, "Okay, you little bi-ch, pull your pants down all the way, and I am going to finish what I started with you," and he already had his pants off and was physically aroused. I refused at first, and then he came inches away from me with the knife at my throat and told me that he was going to kill me right there if I didn't pull my pants down. I started sobbing because he had already raped me once, and I didn't want him to do it again, so I refused to pull my pants down. My stepfather started to yell at me, "Shut up, you stupid little bi-ch! You have to do what I tell you now because your mommy isn't here to stop me, and I'm going to kill you now if you don't pull your pants down right now." Then he shoved the knife right up to

Chapter Two — The Memories I Didn't Know I Had

my face, and he had a terrible, awful look on his face, and there was no doubt in my mind that he was fully intending to kill me if I didn't do what he said. So I thought, *Well, I guess it is better to let him do this to me than to be dead*, and I took my pants off and he raped me. After he was done, he screamed at me that if I told anyone about this, he was going to kill me for sure, "you little bi-ch!"

After he and my uncle had left, I pulled my pants back on and started crying. I went into the house and got in bed. I put my face in the pillow, and I was sobbing for my mother, and I truly wanted to die because this was the most horrible thing that had happened to me. My grandmother came in and tried to talk to me and calm me down, and I just kept crying and saying I wanted my mother. She very sarcastically told me that women have been having babies for hundreds of years and then left the room. She had not made me feel better at all, and I had no idea what she was even talking about. I managed to quiet myself down, and I cried myself to sleep that night. The next morning my stepfather told me to

I Choose Life

get in his car again. I was emotionally numb and checked out at this point, and I just did what he said. Again, I closed my eyes and pretended to be asleep so there was no chance for him to talk to me, and I was wishing that I had already died so that this "nightmare" would be over. The combination of all of the traumas over the past two years had left me totally stripped of any feelings of power to take care of myself or have my voice be heard, and I just wanted to be dead because then I would be away from my stepfather once and for all, and I wouldn't have to worry about what his next move was going to be, and then I would be free from the incredible pain I had inside from what had happened to me.

It took seventeen years and a lot of work for me to be able to remember that I had wished I was dead when this happened. I had emotionally disassociated from this and remembered it like I was watching a movie with me in it at first. The reality is that it was in my body whether I acknowledged the feeling or not, and my body remembered that I had felt this way for thirty-nine years. I was

Chapter Two — The Memories I Didn't Know I Had

happy that I was finally able to feel this because, as Louise Hay says, "What you feel, you can heal." (7) I also realized that I had another level of anger around this death wish in me, and I was still reacting to some situations with this anger, and now I would be able to work on healing the emotional hurt and let go of the behaviors that were causing me problems.

We ended up back at our house in Maryland, and I remember walking into the house and collapsing on the floor. I can only imagine what a mess I was when I walked into the house. My mother was also a victim in this incident, and I don't think she ever forgave herself for the things that happened to me and took full responsibility and blamed herself in her own mind for letting this happen to me. My mom came immediately, picked me up, put me on the couch, and put a blanket over me. The next morning, she came and whispered in my ear that she called me in sick for school and to pretend that I was asleep until my stepfather had gone to work and my sisters had gone to school. Then my mom came and got me out of bed, and we went and sat in a La-Z-Boy rocker/recliner, rocking on and off for most of the day. I stayed home from school for three days, and then one morning my mom came and told me that the school was asking strange questions, and I would have to go to school the next day. My mom asked me if I could do that, and I told her that I would. I went to school and had a terrible stomachache all day, but I managed to make it through the day, and I was actually happy to be someplace that I knew was safe from my stepfather.

After I remembered this, I was horrified at how my mom must have felt when she had come home from the grocery store and saw my stepfather's car gone and then found out I wasn't home either. This was a long time before cell phones were invented, and I can't even imagine the heartache and agony that she went through not knowing what was going on or where we had gone or what was going to happen. I doubt that she called the police because of the other incidents that had happened, and she would have been afraid of losing the other kids

Chapter Two — The Memories I Didn't Know I Had

---

and the possibility of going to jail. So she just had to wait and worry until we got back home to Maryland. As I worked on this with several counselors, I realized that in this instance, I might have lost the battle, but I was not going to lose the war with my stepfather for being able to get free from his obsession with having total control over me.

Later, after I had emotionally healed some more, this incident became a very sad image in my mind of my stepfather (a tall, big-boned, 220-pound man), who had felt so desperate to have power and control over a tiny and dainty ten-year-old girl that he went to such extreme measures to prove to me (from his point of view) that he was totally in control of what I did. From my point of view, it just made me become very aware of needing to keep myself safe from my stepfather no matter what, and I was always aware of where he was in the house and what type of a mood he was in.

After that incident, my sister Marie got moved into my old bedroom, and I got moved into the other room

I Choose Life

with Anne. We had to sleep in a double bed together, and I didn't care at all because that room felt safe to me, and I was happy that I didn't have to sleep in the "faraway" room anymore. Then I realized that since I had put up such a fight with my stepfather, he had moved Marie into that room so he could abuse her instead of me. I felt guilty about this, and two counselors told me many times that, at ten years old, I had no way of knowing what was going on with Marie and my stepfather. Marie had a different personality than I did, and I doubt that she fought back like I had done just because of that. A counselor told me that there was also a good chance that Marie had liked the attention since there were five children competing for attention in our house. Then I remembered that over the years my stepfather had taken Marie shopping for clothes, and he had never taken me or Anne. I had been jealous that Marie was getting extra clothes at the time, but I never wanted to go shopping with my stepfather for anything!

I remembered that Kelly had told me that my ten-year old self was a shaman in training and that I would

Chapter Two — The Memories I Didn't Know I Had

eventually bring healing to a lot of people in my own way. It is not too surprising that, after this event, I gained a lot of weight. I was ten years old and weighed 135 pounds—more than what I weigh as a five-foot-three adult now. Fortunately, when I was fourteen years old, my mother offered to go on the Weight Watchers diet with me, and I lost a lot of weight and went back to a normal size for my height. Although there was still some residue of a feeling inside me that I needed to have "more," I managed to keep the weight off.

As I continued to work on my recovery, I learned to cut back on being too busy with activities and trying to do too much stuff to look good on the outside to make up for my residual pain on the inside. I spent more time in meditation daily and allowed myself to get in touch with the "real me" that was still whole and complete regardless of what had happened to my physical body. I started to get more and more in touch with the part of me that was born to be a writer, and I would allow myself regular time to write. This was very therapeutic for me to be able to write the complete truth about what happened to me and to be able to tell the truth about my feelings, and I didn't have to censor anything based on the reaction I was seeing on someone's face when I tried to tell people my story verbally. I can remember coming from a counseling session and recalling the horrified look on the counselor's face and thinking, *How am I supposed to get completely better if the person I am paying to help me is too horrified to hear the whole story?* Something I have learned for sure after twenty-one years in Al-Anon is that none of us is alone in what has happened to us, and by sharing our stories we give others permission to tell the awful, horrifying truth of what has happened to them.

Now the Odd Things Make Sense

My mother eventually got it together and left my stepfather and divorced him, which was huge for her, and Marie was the only daughter who kept in touch with my stepfather after the divorce. Then I realized that the counselor was probably right that Marie had liked the extra attention

Chapter Two — The Memories I Didn't Know I Had

---

from my stepfather. When I was about twenty-five, I got the idea that something had been going on sexually between Marie and my stepfather, and I called Marie and asked her if that might have happened. At first she didn't say anything at all, and then she got a little mad at me and told me that nothing had happened. Then she started calling me names and got me so upset that I got off the phone. A counselor told me that Marie's reaction would be normal for someone who was sexually abused and wasn't ready to talk about it. Then I remembered my college roommate, Janet, visiting us for Thanksgiving one year instead of traveling home to St. Louis from Williamsburg. Janet had asked me when we got back to William and Mary if there was something going on between my stepfather and Marie. I asked her why she said that, and she told me that my stepfather had been looking at Marie very oddly, and she had the feeling that there was something going on between the two of them. I told her that I didn't think there was anything going on, and she didn't seem totally convinced that I was telling her the truth.

I Choose Life

I remembered that after I had gotten my driver's license when I was sixteen, I had gone upstairs to see if Marie wanted to go shopping with me. It was a Saturday afternoon, and the door to her room was closed. I asked her through the door, and she told me that she didn't want to go. I tried to open the door to her room to talk to her in person, but the door kept slamming shut, and I became totally determined to get that door open. Finally I pushed so hard that I could see my sister's hand with a brush in it hitting my hands and arms to close the door, and I also saw a naked man's body from the waist down that was ready to have sex. Then the door slammed shut. This lasted about ten minutes, and I can remember standing outside that door with my hands and arms all red and scratched up from her hitting me with a brush, and I was thinking, *What just happened? I only asked her if she wanted to go shopping.* When I told this to a counselor, he told me that of course my stepfather was the naked man, and it was his strength behind the door that I had been fighting with. Another time my mom asked me if I had

Chapter Two — The Memories I Didn't Know I Had

heard Marie scream during the night because my room was next to hers. I told her I didn't hear it, and she told me Marie had screamed and thrown a glass at her bedroom door and had broken the glass. My mom told me that when she got to my sister's room (the opposite end of the house from my mom's bedroom), my stepfather was already in her room. When I told this to a counselor, he told me that Marie had been throwing the glass at my stepfather to try to keep him out of her room. The counselor was sure with no doubts at all that my stepfather had been sexually abusing her. Then I remembered a number of times when we were getting ready to go to school in the morning that my mom had been trying everything she could to get Marie out of bed, and Marie was fighting my mom and saying she wanted to stay in bed. My mom was saying it was because Marie had stayed up too late, but I figured out that those days were probably after my stepfather had been in her room the night before, and since Marie wasn't going to tell the truth about our family "secret," she was claiming to be too tired to go to school

I Choose Life

instead. Marie had gotten accepted to go to Harvard but decided she did not want to be that far away from home and wanted to go to school in Virginia.

When Marie had finished her freshman year of college at Virginia Te ch in Virginia, she called me at my mother's house and started crying and telling me that she wasn't going to come home if my stepfather was there. I talked to Marie for a little while, and she told me that she had been talking to a counselor at college, and the counselor told her to call home and tell us she wasn't coming home unless my stepfather wasn't there. I told my mom what Marie had said on the phone to me, and it seemed to be out of the blue to me, but now it makes perfect sense. My mother looked at me and said, "That's it. I am getting a divorce because I am not going to lose my kids because of him." A counselor told me that my mom would have lost all three of her daughters as adults if she had stayed married to my stepfather. My mother only had a high school education and was a C student, and she knew she wouldn't be able to make much money to feed all of us, so

Chapter Two — The Memories I Didn't Know I Had

this was a tremendous act of courage on her part to risk losing literally everything if she left my stepfather and got a divorce. While my mother did not lose everything, we went through a total change of lifestyle, and she never financially recovered from that.

I include pictures of me when I was four years old, ten years old, thirty-five years old, and fifty-three years old, and it is pretty obvious that something terrible happened to the beautiful little four-year-old by the time she was ten. My journey has been to get myself back to the natural joy and happiness of that four-year-old I was before my stepfather abused me, and I had lost big and important parts of my soul.

My Destiny

In January 2008, I had a Jyotish astrology (astrology from India—Science of Light) reading from a man, Brent, whom I met at the Chopra Center. Even though I had taken Western astrology classes with Blake, I had never had an official reading done by him and never really felt any desire to have one. I heard Brent give a presentation during a weeklong meditation retreat at the Chopra Center, and after about five minutes of hearing him talk, I knew with certainty that I needed to have a reading done by him, no matter how much it cost. At some point in the first fifteen minutes of talking to him about my astrology chart, he said, in a very matter-of-fact way, that I had been sexually abused. I told him that I had been, and he told me it was very obvious in my chart and that it was an experience I was meant to have in this lifetime. He asked me if it had been my father, and I told him that it was my stepfather. He said that made sense from my chart and that all of my siblings had been negatively impacted by my stepfather ,and that was why we all lived far away from each other, which made a lot of sense to me. He also told me that my dharma a Sanskrit word meaning "purpose in life," was to be a spiritual teacher, to write spiritual books, and that I would be a good public speaker. Brent told me that I would be very well respected because of "good karma" I had brought with me from other lifetimes

Chapter Two — The Memories I Didn't Know I Had

---

and that it was a good choice for me to get certified as a meditation teacher at the Chopra Center.

Healing My Shame

I had a huge amount of shame around all of these memories and also around having had a nervous breakdown, like I was truly crazy and something was really mentally wrong with me if I had had one. It also did not help because Anne kept telling everyone in my family not to believe me because I had been on the psych ward in the hospital, and everyone there was crazy. My kids grew up hearing her say this to the rest of my family when I wasn't there, and she brainwashed both of them to believe that I was really crazy. This only added to my shame of what had happened to me, and I did not have any way to prevent it or protect myself when I was only nine years old. It helped me a lot when my counselor reframed this as a "breakthrough" and not a "breakdown." Even after I told this to my mom and Anne, I could hear them talking about me behind my back. They never accepted this as a breakthrough and kept telling people I was crazy since I had been on the psych ward. My Mom was in denial about what had happened and couldn't admit to anyone that these things had occurred while I was growing up, and Anne took her word for it. Joe told me that my mom and Anne had both told him this sexual abuse wasn't true; Anne was five years old, and I really wonder how Joe thinks she could possibly know everything that did or did not happen in our house then.

Yet I know after many years in Al-Anon meetings that one of the definitions of denial is "*don't even know I'm lying*" because you lie to yourself and others so much that you believe the lies you have told yourself. Then your life becomes those lies. From my point of view, they both lied to Joe, and yet I know it was out of denial and a need to protect themselves from having to look at this as being true and not being strong enough or ready to deal with the truth. With so much challenge and opposition from my own family, it has become very clear to me why so many victims have kept quiet or been convinced that they

Chapter Two — The Memories I Didn't Know I Had

are making things up or that it never happened. As the victim of this abuse, I can attest that it was bad enough that it happened, and it was like putting salt in the wound for them to be denying it and continuing to claim that I was the crazy one. I reached a point where I started telling them very little about my continuing emotional work and healing because it was pretty clear to me that they didn't understand at all what I was going through.

There were a few people at Al-Anon meetings who were brave enough to talk about the sexual abuse in their homes while growing up, and they became my support system, as well as my counselors, who never doubted that what I was telling them was true. They knew that the things I was telling them were "normal" for someone who is a survivor of sexual abuse, and yet most of the world is completely uneducated about this type of abuse, and very few people are willing to talk about it at all. I have had to learn ways to weave it into my Al-Anon story so that I don't end up with a room full of people all looking at the floor, and then there are almost no comments at the end of the meeting

I Choose Life

because no one wants to talk about it. The irony of this to me is that at a teenage drug and alcohol and treatment center, it is common knowledge that 90 percent of them have been sexually abused, and this is dealt with as a normal part of their treatment. In women's juvenile detention facilities, it is also common knowledge that almost all of them have been sexually abused. Oprah had a show with two hundred male sexual abuse survivors holding a picture of themselves at the ages they had been when their abuse had occurred. (8) When I saw the pictures of those men and how old they were when their abuse first started, I realized that sexual abuse probably starts earlier for boys, most likely because their anatomy makes it easier to sexually abuse them at a younger age than girls. Yet, regardless of being male or female, the shame and devastation from the sexual abuse is the same and gets compounded when no one is willing or able to let you talk about it openly.

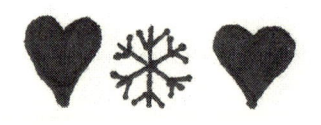

Chapter Three — Healing Myself from the Inside Out

After I was home from the hospital and had found some counselors to work with me, I felt like I spent many days walking around in a sort of a fog because I had no idea of who I was anymore. I had gone through a period of figuring out what I like to wear and do when I was growing up, but now it felt like all of that had really been fake because I did not remember at that time that I had been sexually abused and all the things that had happened to me. So now my entire world had been turned upside down, and I really had no idea of who I was or what I really wanted out of life except that I wanted to feel better and I wanted to figure out a job that I would like as much as my boss at Marriott headquarters had liked his job when I worked for him.

When I was growing up, my mom would take us shopping to buy something to make us feel better after we had just left the doctor's office, and this was what I had learned from her. I remember driving in my car one day and thinking that I could buy the entire Saks Fifth Avenue store, and it would not make this incredible pain inside of me feel better; there just wasn't enough stuff in the world to make my pain go away. This started me on a serious spiritual quest to find meaning in the pain and suffering I had been through and also find a way to feel better. I bought more Mother Teresa books because reading those always made me feel better. At some point I remember thinking that I needed a spiritual "mother" because my biological mother had done a good job of teaching me and helping me in life until then,

Chapter Three — Healing Myself from the Inside Out

but she did not really believe in church or God, and we had really only gone to church when my grandfather visited us because church was important to him.

Then I started having dreams about Mother Teresa; she would come to me, hold my chin with her right hand, look into my eyes, and tell me, "It is okay, child. I will help you. I am your spiritual mother, and I will guide you for the rest of your life." This really helped me, especially when I had had a rough day or week dealing with Drake or new sobriety. I would wake up in the morning after one of those dream visits from Mother Teresa and think, *I can handle this*, and I would feel good about the new day ahead of me. She is still in my dreams today and is still helping me when I come to life's bumps in the road.

When I learned about archetypes, I knew with absolute clarity that Mother Teresa is an archetype of energy for me. Recently I have had dreams that Mother Teresa is the "Great Mother" riding on a tiger's back helping people. I also kept seeing an image of my mom holding my heart in her hands up to her heart and rocking in a rocking chair at my grandfather's house, looking out the window and watching me gather up and find the thousand pieces of me that were "broken." I started on a quest to find out who I really was since my old definition of who I thought I was had been thrown out the window for good.

Rediscovering the Artist in Me

One day a friend of mine at Al-Anon asked me if I would take a class with her called "The Artist's Way," based on a book by Julia Cameron(9), that was being offered at Ursuline (a local Catholic college). I said okay, and we started the class for six weeks, beginning the following week. This class was life-changing for me because I had never been allowed to embrace the creative, artsy side of myself when I was growing up because my mom would tell me over and over that because I was the "smart" one in our family, that meant I would grow up and make a lot of money and no art classes for me. She made me take very practical classes in high school and would not

Chapter Three — Healing Myself from the Inside Out

let me take any art classes like my sisters were allowed to do.

We did an art project with every class, and I loved doing these. This class was taught by Sister Sarah, a trained art therapist, and I found out from talking to her that I had been doing art therapy with Drake, and I didn't even know it. I was telling her that when Marie was sick, we had the kids paint pictures to take to her in the hospital and that Drake had painted pictures with a lot of pretty colors in them. Then after we were back in Cleveland after she died, all he painted were entire pages of black. I did not think anything of it when the first picture he painted was all black, but when all of them were black, I realized that he was expressing his sadness over Marie's death with this black paint. It was really interesting, years later, when Drake was in the third grade; they wrote short autobiographies about themselves, and the pictures Drake drew for himself when he was four, five, and six years old were all black, and his teacher asked me if black was his favorite color. I told her what I thought it meant since it corresponded with the time when Marie had died and the two years after her death. The teacher looked at me with compassion and a little embarrassment and said, "Oh, I didn't think of that." I told Sister Sarah that he had recently painted a picture with all black and one small spot about the size of a quarter in brown, and I felt like celebrating because he was beginning to heal. Sister Sarah agreed with me and told me that that was what art therapy was all about and that the only art therapy program in Cleveland was taught at Ursuline. Sister Sarah recommended that I meet with the woman in charge of this program to learn more about it. I made an appointment with her, and she wanted me to bring my own original artwork with me because you need to be a trained artist to be an art therapist.

I had made quilts, so I took those with me to show to Sister Kathleen. She asked me what art classes I had taken, and I told her that I had never taken an art class before; she looked at me and told me that my quilts were stunning and that I was already an artist if I had done those

Chapter Three — Healing Myself from the Inside Out

without ever taking an art class. She told me that I would need to take basic art classes to get accepted to the art therapy program, although she had a strong feeling that I would just become an artist once I got in the art classes because my work was beautiful, and she found it amazing that I had done this without any formal training. She told me to take classes at the local community college so it would not cost me a lot of money to see if I liked them or not. Well, I loved those art classes and learning things in a totally different way than I had done when I learned "book" knowledge that you memorize and repeat back on a test. I learned from the other students in the classes and found out about other art classes, and I wanted to take graphic design, which I was really excited about. I also realized that I felt a strong uneasiness within myself as I was processing the emotional traumas I had lived through, and when I sat to draw or paint, that uneasiness was almost gone completely, and it was really the only activity I could do where I would not feel that continual uneasiness and pain inside of me. I absolutely loved graphic design and the projects we had in those classes. I got good grades on my projects, and the teacher commented to me several times that she could not teach anyone to do what I did with color and that I had a true gift with colors. It was interesting to me because putting the colors together was my favorite part of the design process because from my point of view color was the way to make a design pop or not. Putting these colors together was as easy as child's play for me and didn't feel like work at all.

Starting a Daily Journal

Other gifts I received from The Artist's Way class were to start keeping a daily journal that I wrote first thing in the morning with my uncensored impressions right after I woke up. I loved keeping this "morning page" journal and started adding affirmations at the end of my daily writings to help add positive energy to the rest of my day. This helped me change the way I was talking to myself when I had clear affirmations in my mind to take with me throughout the day. Then one day I decided I really

Chapter Three — Healing Myself from the Inside Out

needed to be much nicer about the way I was talking to myself and change the "tapes" running through my head, so I got the idea to start describing myself with at least three positive words from every letter in the alphabet. The first time I tried to do this, the only words I could think of were negative, and I was really surprised at how hard it was for me to think of positive words for every letter in the alphabet and even harder to own those positive qualities for myself. I had never been aware of how many negative messages I had received about myself when I was growing up until I tried to do this exercise. My stepfather was always telling me that I was "bad" and called everyone in our house stupid. One of the counselors I worked with pointed out to me that the person in my home who had done bad things was my stepfather, and since I had been a straight-A student in high school and gone to William and Mary, my stepfather was the "stupid" one compared to me.

I stuck with the process of changing the "tapes" that I had running through my mind because, deep down inside myself, I knew that being able to own these positive qualities was absolutely essential for me to start feeling better. I would mentally work on these lists in the car when I was driving back and forth to take my kids to school and their activities. At first I only could think of one or two positive words for each letter, and now I have a very long list with many choices for each letter except for X. This turned out to be a really life-changing practice for me, and now I can tell someone with no problem or hesitation at all that I am articulate, brave, compassionate, dependable, energetic, fun, etc. This was incredibly hard for me, and I had to really work on this practice every day for almost two years before I could begin to own these qualities even a little bit. I had a really difficult and hard time with the words "attractive" and "beautiful" because I did not feel like I was attractive or beautiful at all, especially with the sexual abuse because knowing that about myself made me feel like I was "damaged" goods forever because of that bad experience. At some point after about two years

Chapter Three — Healing Myself from the Inside Out

of working on this list of positive words, I remember looking in the bathroom mirror and seeing myself as a pretty woman for the first time in my life. I started to cry because my stepfather had made me feel so ugly that I had never even realized that I was attractive. Then I cried even harder because no one had ever told me that I was attractive when I was growing up, and I didn't just start to look that way overnight; I had been born beautiful and had been made to feel really ugly. This was a huge breakthrough for me to be able to start to see the beauty I was born with.

After I could own these positive qualities about myself then I was able to sincerely compliment and point out these positive qualities in other people. I had to be able to own them for myself first before I could sincerely give any of them away in a compliment to someone else. Now there is really no question in my mind that these qualities are true about me and who I am. I have done this as an exercise at Al-Anon meetings that I have been in charge of, and it is fun to see how many positive words we can come up with as a group, and it is also really interesting how many people come up to me at the end of the meeting and tell me that they cannot believe those good things about themselves, and they really appreciated my doing that exercise. Now that I like myself a lot more and can see many positive qualities about myself, it is getting hard to remember not liking myself. What a change!

Something else that helped me was to start allowing myself to have "artist's dates" with myself when I would go and spend a day or afternoon doing or learning about something I wanted to learn. This can also be taking myself to a movie I want to see or going to see something at the museum or visiting a place I have wondered about but had never seen before. This has opened up a lot of enriching experiences for me and allowed me to nurture parts of myself that had been totally neglected when I was growing up. I don't always do something every week, like Julia recommends in her book, but I do take myself on these on a regular basis.

Chapter Three — Healing Myself from the Inside Out

Learning More about Mother Teresa

Another gift I received from The Artist's Way was talking to Sister Sarah at lunch one day and asking how I could be able to meet Mother Teresa in person. I had never cared at all about meeting anyone famous, and yet I wanted to meet her in person if it was possible. Sister Sarah looked at me and was really surprised that I said this to her. She told me that Mother Teresa was almost as hard to see in person as the pope, but something the nuns are encouraged to do in their monasteries is to learn as much as they can about spiritual people who inspire them. Sister Sarah told me to start a collection of books on Mother Teresa and read all of them because if I was that attracted to her then I had something in common with her and her spiritual mission in this lifetime.

Mother Teresa grew up in an affluent family and then worked with people in extreme poverty. I grew up in a very middle-class family and now lived in an affluent area with extreme spiritual poverty. I had a hard time with most of the people I met because a lot of them seemed very shallow to me—very preoccupied with their material success and treating other people badly because their stuff and money were more important to them than other people or their feelings. This was very true in my ex-husband's family; they were very sarcastic to each other and said mean things to each other as a way of communicating. The word "sarcasm" in Greek means to "tear flesh," and that is what it felt like to me when I was around them—they were ripping each other, as well as me, apart with their words. These were some of the "pieces" I was collecting: healing from the bitter sarcasm of my ex-husband and his family.

I started collecting as many books as I could about Mother Teresa and even found a few videos about her that I bought and watched. I have about sixty-five books about Mother Teresa, and reading them has definitely changed me and the way I look at the world.

Learning about the Bible

Since I was really loving all the books about Mother Teresa, I decided that I wanted to learn more about the Bible because I had never learned anything about the

Chapter Three — Healing Myself from the Inside Out

stories in the Bible while I was growing up. I signed up for a class at my church called Disciple, which was a thirty-six-week class that covered 85 percent of the Bible. (10) Students end up reading 85 percent of the Bible by the time they are done with the class. This class was also life-changing for me because the reading started out as an assignment, with about three hours of reading each week, and, at some point, God came alive for me in those pages, and I couldn't wait to get to my assignments so I could spend more time with God.

This Disciple class helped me understand the problems in my family of origin much better. My grandfather had lived his life as a beautiful example of Christian living, in contrast to my own mother and stepfather and the way they lived their lives. The more I learned, the clearer it became to me that the problem in my alcoholic family of origin was that God wasn't really there. I figured out that we had only gone to church when my grandfather visited us as my mom's attempt to make him think we were active and involved in a church. There could not

I Choose Life

have been anything further from the truth. I loved learning the stories in the Bible and liked that they gave me a new way to look at things—one that matched and complemented the things that I learned at Al-Anon meetings. Some of the verses became my absolute favorites and helped me put my life and breakthrough in a totally different perspective.

The first verse that really helped me was in the book of Genesis; this is the first book in either the Hebrew or Christian scriptures. It is from the story of a man named Joseph, whose brothers sold him into slavery because they were jealous of him. Joseph worked his way up and had a gift for interpreting dreams that got him into a top position of authority. There was a famine, and his brothers came to him for help but were afraid that he wouldn't help them because of what they had done to him. Joseph replied to them: "But as for you, ye thought evil against me; but God meant it unto good" (Genesis 50:20). Joseph did not hold it against them and saw the event as something God had used to bring a lot of good to him. This

Chapter Three — Healing Myself from the Inside Out

was life-changing for me because I knew as soon as I read this verse that something really good would end up coming out of the trauma I had gone through as a child, and there was no doubt about this in my mind. This gave me a powerful new way to look at my stepfather and what he had done to me. He raped me twice, almost killed me twice, and committed a murder in front of my face. Instead of wallowing in self-pity about what had happened, I could choose to see that God intended good to come from these experiences in my life. Now I am telling my story so that others who have been through horrendous and traumatic experiences and abuse in their lives can have hope and heal. One of the real gifts from these experiences is that I have had to work for years on forgiveness for the many wrongs done to me, and that has forced me to have more and more contact with God.

When I started going to Al-Anon in 1992, I believed in God, but I did not really have a time-tested relationship with Him like I do now. I have come to rely on God in a very meaningful way, and I know that God has "got my back." As the years have gone by, God has given me little miracles to help me see that He was at work in my life, and these little miracles motivated me to keep on working until all of my grievances and resentments felt completely better in my body. This has taken a long time, and I can understand why a lot of people have given up without the results they wanted. It takes a lot of endurance to hang in there until some of the wounds begin to heal. What I have learned is that the bigger the injury I suffered, the longer it took for me to really forgive and begin to feel better. Then there were a lot of smaller injuries that I needed to deal with once I had finished with the bigger stuff. I also became aware that I was really mad at my biological father for dying and leaving me vulnerable to the attacks by my stepfather. I knew this was ready to heal when I began dreaming about my four-year-old self and the behaviors that she possessed in my current life. I would need to redefine myself (again) if I got rid of these behaviors, and yet, because of my dreams and other recovery work, I was ready to do this. My original wound was ready to heal, and I was ready to learn new skills and find a new career for myself.

Many Different Bible Translations

There were many, many Bible verses that I came to love from this study, but there were several themes that have rippled into almost every facet of my life seventeen years later. I loved hearing people read from their different versions of the Bible and bought some of them that I really liked. I probably have about a dozen different versions of the Bible, and I really like to read verses in all of the versions when I have the time because there are no perfect translations from the scriptures since a lot of them were written in Aramaic, originally by hand, and there are problems with being certain about what letters the writer intended and also problems with handwriting and determining what was intended. There are also different interpretations of how to modernize the scriptures or translate the same words into English. While it can be a little frustrating that it is not an exact science, I really like

I Choose Life

the variety of the different verses and the many different ways to express the same idea.

The themes that have really rippled out into my day-to-day life are: good can come from suffering and pain; God talks to us in our dreams; God knows our thoughts and helps us transform our thinking; God helps us find a new song; God looks at our hearts; beauty is God's creation; and God wants us to choose life.

Good Can Come from Suffering

I first started to learn about good coming out of suffering at Al-Anon, but then I learned even more about this from reading the Bible during the Disciple class's Bible study. I went on to take Disciple 3, Remember Who You Are, and then I took a nine-month class called Christian Believer. (11) I taught Disciple 3 one year and participated in a neighborhood weekly Bible study for six or seven years.

There are many examples in the Bible where good comes out of suffering and pain and then brings resurrection. The story of Job is a perfect illustration of this.

Chapter Three — Healing Myself from the Inside Out

These stories helped me see that having painful life experiences has been part of the human condition for many thousands of years. It also helped me see that the choice of what to do about those experiences is what makes the difference in the long run. I really liked learning to look at things differently and to keep reminding myself that all of my life challenges and difficulties are teaching me things I can't learn another way. They also give me the experience of knowing that many things that were huge challenges at the time made me stronger to deal with other new challenges that came my way later on.

In a number of places, God tells us that He will not give us more than we can handle. Mother Teresa says that when we feel like a challenge is too big for us to take it as a compliment because God thinks we can handle it or He wouldn't let us have the challenge.

God Talks in Our Dreams

The next theme that has rippled through to my everyday life is that God talks to us in our dreams. I have dreams that I remember from many, many years ago, and I liked learning that dreams were a way for God to talk to us. I have heard Deepak Chopra make the comment that "our dreams bring us messages from our soul." That feels like it is a different way of saying the same thing. There is a verse, Numbers 12:6, that says, "Hear now my words: If there be a prophet among you, I the Lord will make myself known unto him in a vision, and will speak unto him in a dream." A very interesting synchronicity just happened as I was writing this. I was listening to music on iTunes on an old laptop and right after I wrote the first sentence of this paragraph, the song "You Make My Dreams Come True" by Hall & Oats started playing. I love it when the timing is so perfect in a way that I could have never planned ahead of time when I turned on my very old iTunes playlist!

Changing My Thinking

Another theme was learning that God knows our thoughts and helps us transform ourselves by changing our thinking and thoughts. In Al-Anon, we talk about "stinking thinking" and how important it is to change the quality of our thoughts because our thoughts have a way of coming true, good or bad. There is a quote from the Buddha: "What you think, you become." This was why I changed the way I was talking to myself because I wanted to become the positive qualities I affirmed to myself and not the negative thinking I had learned in my family when I was growing up. There are a couple of Bible verses about this: "And be renewed in the spirit of your mind; and that ye put on the new man" (Ephesians 4:23-24), "Be not conformed to this world; but be ye transformed by the renewing of your mind" (Romans 12:2).

There are a number of articles available online about the importance of your words and thoughts because of the energy vibration they create within your personal energy field. Thoughts and words have energy, and it is really important to pay attention to the words we tell ourselves and how they do affect what we come to believe to be true about ourselves, and then ripple out into the environment around us. The verse in Psalms 19:14, "Let the words of my mouth, and the meditation of my heart, be acceptable in thy sight, O Lord," and the verse in Psalms 139:14, "I am wonderfully made," remind us that God knew us before we were born and we are wonderfully made for whatever situations or circumstances may come our way during our life journeys.

Affirming positive qualities over and over again to myself eventually allowed me to own those positive qualities, and as I started to be able to own them for myself, I was able to compliment and point out those qualities to other people. I couldn't do this until I could own these for myself first. We cannot give someone else something we don't have to give. This has contributed in a large way to the total transformation that I have gone through in the last eighteen years.

Singing My Song

The next theme that has become significant in all areas of my life is the idea of having a new song to sing. Many of the people who come to Al-Anon for the first time are singing a song of complaining about everything or feeling

Chapter Three — Healing Myself from the Inside Out

sorry for themselves and having a lot of self-pity. There are verses that talk about having a new song: Psalm 144:9, "I will sing a new song unto thee, O God"; Isaiah 12:2, "I will trust, and not be afraid: for the Lord Jehovah is my strength and my song"; Isaiah 30:29, "Ye shall have a song, and gladness of heart"; and Isaiah 42:10, "Sing unto the Lord a new song." Without even knowing that this was one of God's promises to us in the scriptures, I had found a new song for myself when I started singing "Praise the Lord" to myself when I heard music, and it did help me feel better, definitely stronger and much happier when I wasn't spending all of my thoughts on the problems in my life.

In one of the teacher trainings I went to for the Christian Believer class, we were talking about how all of creation naturally "sings" praise to the Creator: birds chirping and singing, the leaves on the trees waving in the wind, flowers growing, bees buzzing around, etc. We are wired to give praise and practice gratitude, and yet many of us have lost this in our everyday lives. This is especially true in alcoholic homes because the nature of the disease of addiction is to be afflicted with negative thinking patterns. Our newspapers and television newscasts have a tendency to reinforce this by only reporting stories that are bad or upsetting instead of having a television newscast that shows only good things that happened in our community and world that day. We can only think one thought at a time, and when we focus our energy on having more positive thoughts, the negative thoughts fall away because we aren't feeding them as much as we are feeding the positive thoughts by singing our new songs.

God Looks at Our Hearts

The next theme that is in all areas of my life now is that God looks at our hearts and the importance of the purity of your heart. In Chinese medicine, the heart is considered the "brain" of the body because the condition of our heart influences all of the thoughts and choices we make. There are scientific studies on the Internet by Heartmath Institute, Rollin McCraty, Director of Research wrote

Chapter Three — Healing Myself from the Inside Out

that: the heart radiates and gives off an electromagnetic field that affects others' moods, attitudes, and feelings whether we are aware of it or not. He included pictures that show how the heart's magnetic field can be measured up to several feet away from the body. He introduced new research showing that the heart is more powerful than the brain. The heart is about 100,000 times stronger electrically and about five thousand times stronger magnetically than the brain. (12) This research affirms what the writers of the scriptures knew thousands of years ago: the condition of your heart affects everything around you and in your life whether you realize it or not.

In 1 Chronicles 28:9, it says, "the Lord searcheth all hearts, and understandeth all the imaginations of the thoughts," and in Luke 6:45, "A good man out of the good treasure of his heart bringeth forth that which is good; and an evil man out of the evil treasure of his heart bringeth forth that which is evil; for out of the abundance of the heart his mouth speaketh." The words that come out of our mouths are directly influenced by the condition of our hearts. By changing the words we tell ourselves, we heal our hearts of the emotional injuries that caused us to tell ourselves negative things about ourselves and about others. In Psalm 27:14, it states, "Be of good courage, and he shall strengthen thine heart."

I saw Brene Brown speak on "Oprah" recently, and she said the word "courage" stems from the Latin word "cor," meaning "heart." The original definition of courage was to share all of yourself, share your whole story, with your whole heart. (13) It is fascinating to me that we do share our whole stories at Al-Anon meetings, and that is how we heal the injuries we have from all of the painful events in our lives. Happiness is a form of courage and can only come from within our hearts.

The scriptures also teach us, in Proverbs 15:13, "By sorrow of the heart the spirit is broken." Sorrow includes the things we hold on to, like grievances, resentments, and regrets, because these things make our hearts heavy and influence our emotional reactions to other people, places, and things.

Embracing the Beauty All around Me

The next theme in all areas of my life is beauty. In Genesis, we learn: "God saw every thing he had made, and, behold it was very good"; Genesis 1:31, "God was happy with everything he had created—including all of us." In Psalm 29:2, we are instructed to "worship the Lord in beauty." Also, in 2 Chronicles 20:21, we are instructed to "Praise the beauty." God created beauty all around us in the stars, the flowers, pretty sunsets, sparkling gemstones, waterfalls, and the natural beauty that is all around us that is part of God's creation, and I believe He made each one of us to be beautiful as well—only it is part of the human condition that we either forget about this or aren't able to see it and appreciate it because we are injured or too distracted and have our focus on other things. I saw a bumper sticker that said, "Feed your heart with beauty," and I thought that it is good for us to be around beauty because it is nurturing to our souls. There is a quote by a famous Persian poet, Rumi: "I have come to bring out the beauty you never knew you had." (14) I think that getting more connected to God (or our Creator or Spirit) helps us to discover beauty within ourselves that we never knew we had. In my own opinion, Be.YOU.ty comes when we are embracing all of who and what we have been born with and that we really like and accept ourselves totally and completely without any hesitation or reservations.

Being Conscious of the Choices I Make

The last theme in all areas of my life is choosing life, and that is why I chose that as the title for this book because that is really the key principle underlying all the rest. In Deuteronomy 30:19, we are told: "I have set before you life and death, blessings and curses. Now choose life, so that you and your children may live." In Ezekiel 37:6, He tells us, "I will cause breath to enter into you, and ye shall live." And Jesus speaking in John 10:10 says: "I am come that they might have life, and that they might have it more abundantly." We are here to have abundant and beautiful lives. God is telling us to choose life when we make choices throughout our day. Once we start choosing life

Chapter Three — Healing Myself from the Inside Out

every day in every way that we can, our lives become better than we could have ever imagined. In Psalm 20:4, "may he grant your heart's desire" tells us God wants us to be happy and to have our heart's wishes fulfilled, and I believe that this is how we are able to experience life abundantly.

Developing My Unique Skills

As I was learning the stories and verses in the Bible and taking myself on "artist's dates" and learning about things I had always wanted to know how to do, I started getting ideas of putting scriptures or quotes on fabric. On this journey, I read books by Ron Roth, a retired Catholic priest who did healing work and had workshops about healing before he died. (15) I went to one of his workshops, and he was talking about how people need to just get started if they ever want to reach their goals and how many people don't ever start because they don't know how to do what they want and they aren't sure where to start. He was encouraging everyone to just start anyway,

I Choose Life

and if you don't like your result then try a different way, and eventually this will evolve as you continue to work on your ideas. So I started playing around with this idea of putting scriptures on fabric by Xeroxing them onto fabric sheets that can go through a computer printer. My first attempts were not at all what I had been expecting them to look like, but I learned from my first experiment and kept trying different ways to do this.

I started making small wall quilts with the Lord's Prayer on them and then embellishing around this with machine embroidery, and I liked the way this turned out, so I made some more of these. Then I started making handbags out of my embellished quilted fabric and found ways to do this that I liked a lot when they were done. I made the fabric picture for the cover of this book from things I learned about along the way. Then I started taking jewelry making classes because I had always wanted to learn how to make jewelry, and then I incorporated some of the jewelry techniques into my little art quilts, and I liked the end result of those as well. All of this started making me feel happier and happier because I was learning things I had always wanted to know how to do and was able to experiment with my own original ideas with these skills. Also, Brene Brown said on "Oprah," "Unused creativity is not benign," making me glad that I had started reconnecting with my creativity in a healthy way as part of my recovery.

Becoming a Reiki Master

I was interested in getting healthier, so I took Reiki training classes and energy healing classes from local teachers. These classes helped me to get a lot more connected to my body and to be able to start developing better habits in how I was taking care of myself every day. One of the energy healers told us that if we were going to be working on other people's bodies that it was important for us to get "bodywork" or some type of massage done on our bodies on a regular basis. I went to get a massage at a resort when we were on vacation, and the massage therapist told me that the muscles around my neck and shoulders were so tight I was going to have a stroke if I didn't start getting a massage every week when I got home. My mom's mother died from a stroke, so this got my attention, and I started checking around for places to get massages when I got home. I didn't want to take the time every week, so I started going every other week for a massage, and this has made a huge difference in my overall wellbeing and helped me to get more connected with being able to feel what is going on in my body physically.

Changing My Spending

I started consciously changing the way I spent my money from buying a lot of things (like my mother had done) to spending money on experiences instead. This has brought me huge growth because making those changes is an easy thing to talk about or think about, but when it came to actually doing it and sticking with it, it was extremely painful for me sometimes. I was really deeply conditioned by my mother about how to spend money, and actually changing that and sticking with it was difficult for me a

Chapter Three — Healing Myself from the Inside Out

lot of the time. Yet something deep down inside of me intuitively knew that I needed to make these changes in order to get my health back and be happier with my life overall. After twenty-one years on my recovery journey, this is one of the changes that have ended up having the biggest ripple effect into every other area of my life.

It is really ironic to me that I am the one who was always working to pay down our bills when I was married, and because of how little money my ex has given me during our divorce, I am the one with really big debt now, and my credit rating has been destroyed because one of the monthly minimum payments is more than one of the checks my ex gives me to live on for two weeks. I had no debt when I got married and it is my goal to get back to living that way now so that I will be able to control all of the financial choices in my life.

Getting Grounded

One Saturday I had planned to take a quilting class about a technique I had been interested in learning, and my good sewing machine broke the Monday before the workshop. I was upset at first, and then I remembered that I had an old one in my basement that I could use for the class while I got the other one fixed. Then the workshop got canceled on Wednesday because the teacher had a personal emergency. I kept thinking to myself that I had made arrangements to have an entire Saturday for myself (which didn't happen very often when my kids were little because of all of their activities that I drove them to – putting approximately twenty-two thousand miles/year on my car), so I started frantically looking for something to do on that Saturday instead. I found out there was a healing class by an energy healer that I had been wanting to meet, so I signed up and went to that class instead. The week before I took this class, I had been to an ear, nose, and throat specialist who had prescribed eight weeks of heavy duty antibiotics for my sinuses and told me that if they didn't clear up in that time, I would have to schedule surgery for my deviated septum.

This class was all about "grounding," how to actually do it, and to be able to feel it in your body and also

Chapter Three — Healing Myself from the Inside Out

about forgiveness work. In a lot of books about healing, you are told to make sure you are grounded or to be well grounded when doing something, but I had never really understood exactly what that meant in practical terms, and I had absolutely no idea what that felt like in my body. The teacher, Dave, showed us that energy comes into our bodies from the feet up to the top of our head and runs up through our chakras (seven energy centers) very much like water going through a hose. Whatever problems or issues we have had in our lives leave holes in this hose and leaves blocks in the chakra around the issue. Everyone has some of these leaks in their energy, and some people have more or bigger holes than others. Since the energy comes into our bodies through our feet into our first chakra, this is really the most important chakra because if there is not a strong flow of energy coming into the hose, there will not be much energy by the time it gets to the top chakras (our brains and connection to Spirit).

We did exercises to strengthen our feet (called "yoga toes" at yoga studios) to help us be able to bring more energy

I Choose Life

into our first chakra and make us more grounded. Then we did some forgiveness work and learned some yoga breathing that is safe to practice on your own time. This was important to learn because some types of yoga breathing will take you into an altered state of consciousness and can be dangerous if you don't know what you are doing. After about an hour and a half of the workshop, I could feel my sinuses starting to move for the first time in weeks, and I was pretty excited at the possibility of being able to avoid surgery. At the end of the class, my sinuses were feeling much better, and I went over to Dave and asked him if I could make an appointment to see him privately; he gave me his card to call him and set this up.

I went to go see Dave three or four times and worked on more forgiveness work from my childhood traumas with him. Dave told me that any time we are afraid (or terrified, like I was) when we are children, we lose our grounding and that this is a big problem if it happens a lot or with a profound trauma in our childhood because that is the time when we are supposed to be safe and

Chapter Three — Healing Myself from the Inside Out

carefree. He told me that I needed to double my walking time from thirty minutes to an hour every day to get my feet and entire energy system stronger. Since I had grown up in a family that didn't exercise, this felt like a big punishment to me. Dave has a PhD in psychology, and when we were working on my forgiveness issues, he told me that my stepfather was a sociopath, and that was why I had had such a hard time with him when I was growing up. The good thing is that we can get the grounding back if we are willing to work at it.

Dave told me not to worry if I needed to get bigger shoes from working to make my feet stronger because most of the people he knew were wearing shoes that were too small for them that were constricting the energy flow from their feet. This was another "choosing life" challenge for me because getting bigger shoes would mean not wearing my small shoes anymore and to only have three pairs of new, bigger shoes for a little while until I could budget for more a little at a time. I decided I would get the bigger shoes because I didn't want surgery, and

I wanted to be really healthy. I did not start the extra walking right away, but when Drake got involved with his own addiction journey in high school, I started doing the extra walking. I had no idea what a big difference it would make, but it made a really big difference. I started to feel a lot better, and it trimmed my body down even though my weight stayed the same on the scale.

Dave's philosophy was to be "rooted and grounded in love." The next week as part of my Bible study I was doing at the time, I read a verse from Ephesians 3:17-19: "that being rooted and grounded in love, ye may be able to be filled with all the fullness of God." It was amazing to me that these instructions were in the Bible a long time ago, and Dave had taught me a practical way to do this.

Chakras and Colors

I went to another energy healing workshop about the chakras, and the woman teaching it was telling us that it was important to have all of the colors of the chakras in our lives. They could either be in our clothing or our living

Chapter Three — Healing Myself from the Inside Out

environment, but it was important to have all of them, and she told us to look in our closets when we got home and see if we were missing any colors; that would help us know which chakras to work on first. I went home, and I had all of the colors in my closet except orange. I had never realized this or known this about myself before, although I did know that I thought I hated orange for a long time. One day when I was out on a longer walk, I remembered that my stepfather's car was orange when he had abducted me from our house in Maryland and then had raped me in South Carolina. Then I was thinking, *No wonder I hate orange* and at the same time realized this was another place I needed to heal if I wanted to get really healthy. I bought a piece of jewelry that had some orange in it, and that was the best I could do at first. Now I have a lot of orange in my closet, and I even have an orange handbag that I like a lot.

I read recently that Paramahansa Yogananda thought orange was the color of our souls. (16) I was totally out of touch with my soul when I started going to Al-Anon, and it is really interesting that my stepfather had an orange Volkswagon Beetle, and he was the primary reason that I had lost large pieces of my soul as a child.

Discovering Dream work

I took a quilting class at the Orange Arts Center near my house and entered my finished quilt into the yearly art show they have. I was pleasantly surprised when they called me and told me that I had won an Award of Excellence for art, and they were going to put my name on a plaque that hung in the Art Center. They asked me to come to a ceremony they were having as part of the art show. The next Al-Anon meeting I went to, I was talking to a friend of mine who is an accomplished painter and told her I won this award and a blue ribbon. She was telling me to take pictures of it with a professional camera and was really helpful telling me about the steps of what to do as an artist. She and I became friends, and one Wednesday in the summer she came up to me and told me she had been to the best workshop over the weekend

Chapter Three — Healing Myself from the Inside Out

about conscious dreaming and that I would love it and had to go the next time the teacher, Robert Moss, was in Cleveland. She told me to buy his book and read it until I was able to go to a workshop.

I was leaving early the next morning for a vacation in Hatteras, North Carolina, with the rest of my family, but we were going to stop in Williamsburg, Virginia, on the way, so I thought I would look at the bookstore there. I went to the Barnes and Noble bookstore in Williamsburg, and they had one copy of *Conscious Dreaming* by Robert Moss (17), which I bought to take with me to the beach.

Paying Attention to My Dreams

I knew the book would be about dreams, but I wasn't really sure what it was going to be about specifically, and I had never heard of "dream work" before. I had a little bit of quiet time the next afternoon at the hotel, so I started to read this book. Robert was talking about the importance of "catching" and writing down your dreams when you first wake up in the morning. I felt pretty amazed as I was reading this because we were going to be staying in a beach house we had stayed in five times before and were going back again because we really liked the house, which was decorated with mermaids all over it. The name of the house was the "Dreamcatcher," and I had never understood until I was reading Robert's book what this term meant.

I contacted Robert by email after I read his book and mentioned staying in the "Dreamcatcher" house in Hatteras, and he emailed me back that he had some friends who had just returned from having a private retreat in this same house—the magic of connecting with the dream world was already happening, and I felt inspired to follow my dreams even more.

I started writing down my dreams every morning after I read Robert's book and really liked the process of recapitulating my dreams right when I got up. When I was taking my kids to school, and we all had to get up and going much earlier, I would use a little pad of paper to write down a very quick outline of my dream and then drove my kids to school. After I got home, I would get my

Chapter Three — Healing Myself from the Inside Out

outline and write out the full dream in a larger notebook where I could keep all of my dreams together. I had been doing this for three or four months before Robert came back to Cleveland for a weekend workshop. I loved sharing dreams in the group and using the lightning dream work process that Robert developed. I met some really interesting people by connecting with them through the exercises we did at the workshop. I met a woman who dreams about mermaids and was talking to her about some of my mermaid dreams. After this discussion about mermaids, I realized that that was the other thing that was magical about the Dreamcatcher house—it was decorated with mermaids, and I was a "mermaid dreamer" and had not even known this about myself when I stayed there. I feel pretty certain that I am a kindred spirit with the owner of the house because of the mermaids all over it and its name.

Dreams of Power

I learned that the dreams I had about Drake that I could remember even though I never wrote them down were dreams of power. They gave me the strength and clarity to hang in there with Drake because I knew, without a doubt in my mind, that he was supposed to live with me because of those dreams.

Robert encouraged us to go back and look through our dream titles for the last six months or a year and see if there were any common themes or topics coming up repeatedly. When I did this, I realized that I had dreamt about making jewelry and handbags almost a year before I had actually started making these things in physical reality. I had even drawn patterns from my dreams in my notebook that I had used in my handbags that I made later. It was pretty amazing that I had been programmed and had "downloaded" these ideas from my dreams long before I had manifested them in physical reality!

Honoring My Dreams

I learned that dreams help to reconnect us with our souls and to find pieces of our soul we have lost through trauma or heartbreak. I also learned that "spirit guides"

Chapter Three — Healing Myself from the Inside Out

and animals can show up in our dreams and that we can honor them by taking some kind of action. This can be something very simple like writing a poem or drawing a picture about the dream. I had famous people from long ago showing up like Joan of Arc (18) and Sitting Bull (19), so I did research and read books about both of them. I learned that Sitting Bull had been the one responsible for Custer's last stand and that Sitting Bull was the chief of the "strong hearts" in his tribe. The strong hearts were the ones who could be teased, poked, and harassed and would not get upset but stay calm in response to whatever others were doing to try to upset them. The strong hearts were the only ones allowed to lead the tribe into a battle because only someone who could keep a completely calm mind and body would make good decisions during the fighting. I decided that I wanted to be able to have a strong heart after reading and learning about Sitting Bull.

I learned that Sitting Bull liked duck feathers because ducks and their feathers are impervious to water and wind, and they let things roll off their backs just like drops of water. My family room has a collection of ducks on the fireplace mantle. In some subtle way, I had picked up on the strength of the ducks a long time ago and had never even realized it until I learned about Sitting Bull. The neatest thing about all of this to me is that my dreams guided me to things that were helpful for me and helped bring healing to me for things I did not understand before. Working with my dreams started the process of becoming more integrated with my inner life, matching my outside life in physical reality more than I ever had before. I felt much more complete, and my life became incredibly interesting as I continued working with my dreams and learning more and more about myself from the inside out.

As we bring back the pieces of our souls that have been missing, our eyes start to sparkle and shine more as we become more whole and complete. In the two adult pictures of me that I included in this book, you can see the difference between how dull my eyes looked when I was

Chapter Three — Healing Myself from the Inside Out

younger and was missing many pieces of my soul and didn't know it and then how bright I am now that I have done a lot of work at reclaiming all of the missing pieces of my soul. (These pictures are located in Appendix A of this book.) My mother's sadness is very obvious in these pictures – even when she was at the beach having fun. I didn't know it for a long time, but the image of my mom watching me gather up my thousand pieces was actually her watching me gather up the pieces of my soul that were missing.

I emailed the image of my mom holding my heart and rocking in a rocking chair to Robert, and he told me he wished me good luck in healing my "broken heart." I had never thought of it this way before, but I realized that my heart had been broken many, many times from big and little hurts that I had gone through during my lifetime.

Past-Life Memories

I also realized as I continued to work with my dreams that, when I was in the hospital, I had some things that were breaking through from some past lives. I remembered

I Choose Life

one day in the hospital when the nurses were talking to me and asking me if I knew where I was, and I had responded to them in fluent French. I do not speak fluent French in my waking life, but I did in the hospital, and when I was in the hospital I knew exactly what I was telling them. I talked for a few minutes, and then I started screaming at the nurses in French, "Guillaume est le trickster! Guillaume est le trickster!" I said this over and over again, probably about twenty times, and I was really angry and feeling very deeply hurt because there had been betrayal by someone named Guillaume.

I did not grow up Catholic and did not know anything about any of the saints except for what some of their names were. I had three or four dreams about Joan of Arc, so I got a book about her and read it. I was really amazed when I got to the end of the book and found out that the experts are not 100 percent sure who betrayed Joan of Arc, but the one most experts think probably did it was named Guillaume. There is very little doubt in my mind that she was, in fact, betrayed by someone named Guillaume.

Chapter Three — Healing Myself from the Inside Out

At a weeklong workshop with Robert, I had a shamanic journey experience where I learned that Guillaume had been connected to my stepfather in this lifetime and realized that my stepfather had been my adversary in more than one lifetime, and that was part of his extreme anger with me in this lifetime and probably why he had almost killed me twice. When the movie *Cloud Atlas* with Tom Hanks (20) came out, I was really happy to see this past-life concept illustrated so the general public could start to understand about past lives and how they affect our current lives.

Living with a Terrorist

I was forty-eight years old before I figured out that I had lived with a killer in my house from the time I was seven until I was twenty. I have had dreams about how my stepfather tricked my mother and told her that he had our best interests at heart (mine and my two sisters'). In reality, my stepfather was a pedophile who saw three little girls he could take advantage of and abuse. In the biggest dream about this, my stepfather was a wolf in sheep's clothing and a total con artist with my mom about what his real intentions were and why he wanted to marry her. My mom told me that most of the men that she met were not interested in her at all once she told them that she had three little children, so then it made a lot of sense why my stepfather wasn't bothered by this.

I learned from a counselor that my stepfather was a bigot and took it as a matter of total fact and truth that all African-Americans were just "dumb niggers" and should be treated harshly and inhumanely like they treated the animals on the farm where he grew up. It pained me greatly to see him kick an older African-American woman just like it was no different than stepping on an ant. I had a dream about naming my book *There's a Killer in My House—Someone Please Believe Me!* I saw an image of a dark cover with a switchblade knife and a hangman's noose. I know this came to me because of the horrors I was telling people and my counselor about and that other people didn't believe that this had happened to me, and

Chapter Three — Healing Myself from the Inside Out

I wasn't in a mental institution or barely functioning, which is what the counselors would expect for someone who had been through this type of trauma as a child.

On the outside, my stepfather seemed like a very respectable person: an officer in the navy who got up and went to work every day and paid his bills. He never got arrested for anything, and he appeared to be very normal. Yet the reality from my point of view is that this man was a terrorist in every sense of the word. Over time, I decided to choose another title for my book and use a different picture for the cover because I wanted to be able to offer encouragement and hope to other abuse survivors who couldn't get anyone to believe them or be willing to talk about this with them either.

Throughout this process, there have been a number of times that I have gotten really mad at God for continuing to give me such big challenges over and over again. Someone said to me, "That which doesn't kill us makes us stronger." While I like the idea of getting stronger, I sometimes got even madder at God because I kept

I Choose Life

thinking, *You know, God, I never wanted to be Superman. Stop it!* This was another form of feeling sorry for myself, and sometimes I was just plain tired from all the challenges in my life.

Chapter Four — My Healing Really Takes Off

I was blessed to have a grandfather who totally adored me. Kelly, the psychic I met when Marie was dying, told me the first time I met her that I was his favorite only he never told me because he didn't want to hurt or upset my sisters and brothers; I think deep down I knew this anyway. He was my mother's father, and he made me feel like I could do anything. He loved me deeply, and I always knew it; even though he never spoke those words to me, there was never a doubt in my mind that my grandfather loved me. Since I spent a lot of time with him after my father died, he became my substitute father, and in my mind there was no doubt that my grandfather was a good man – safe. As I continued to grow up, my stepfather became my image of a bad man – scary.

I had dreams of my Grandfather on his hands and knees beside his bed, praying for me after these traumatic events occurred to me. My grandfather started crying while he was praying for me, and in the dream I could feel his heartbreak when he saw me after the last incident had happened at my stepfather's family farm. In the dream, I knew that my grandfather's prayers for me during that time helped me survive and gave me the strength later on to heal and find all of my missing thousand pieces. Never underestimate the power of your prayers for someone else's wellbeing. My grandfather did not live long enough to see my healing happen, and yet I have no doubts at all that his prayers so long ago have given me the energy to

Chapter Four — My Healing Really Takes Off

keep on keeping on as I worked on myself to find all of my missing pieces.

Something we talk about often in Al-Anon is about how things in the world often happen in "God's time" and not in our "own time," and because of this we misunderstand and think that God didn't hear us or listen to us, and really it was a matter of timing. There is a Mother Teresa quote that I love: "To pray is to allow God to come alive in us." (21) The end results of my grandfather's prayers so long ago and my song prayer, "Praise the Lord," have allowed me to experience God's coming alive in me, and I am profoundly grateful for my grandfather's prayers even though he did not live long enough to see the manifestation of his prayers come true in my life.

Another quote from Mother Teresa, "Everything starts with prayer,"(22) came to have a lot significance for me as I realized and became aware that all of my healing, all of my remembering, and all of my knowing what I wanted to do and liked to do had started with a very simple three-word prayer, "Praise the Lord." Sometimes it is the smallest changes that end up changing your life forever, and my decision to change my thinking turned out to have a huge result on the rest of my life. There is very little doubt in my mind that my inspiration to start my "singing" prayer practice came from God and going to Al-Anon meetings.

Going to the Chopra Center

I loved working with my dreams and went to all of the advanced Dream Teacher workshops that Robert offered. Since I like to keep adding on to what I already know, I was starting to look around for what else I would want to do for a week since I had figured out how to fit in a week away from my family. I had three different dreams with Deepak Chopra in them where I was sitting there listening to him talk to a group of people. I had a dream that I needed to be with more eagles so I would be hanging out with people who were like me.

When I had been on my way to one of Robert's workshops in Cleveland, I ran into my neighbor whose daughter was my kids' favorite babysitter. I told her I

Chapter Four — My Healing Really Takes Off

was going to a dream workshop, and she wanted to come also. After the workshop was over, my neighbor came over to me and said that if I liked the dream workshop, I needed to go to a Deepak Chopra workshop because he was amazing. I told her I wasn't sick because I had seen Deepak on "Oprah" talking about his *Perfect Health* book (23), and I had gotten the impression that all of his workshops were for people with health problems. She told me that he had other things also, and, about a month later, there was a Chopra Center catalog in my mailbox (sent to me from my neighbor) that had a list of all of the workshops that they had. Many of them were about health and healthcare, so I picked out one called Seduction of Spirit, which was a weeklong meditation retreat at Paradise Point Resort in San Diego, California. I had no idea what it was going to be like or what we would do, but I was looking forward to it since I had read a number of Deepak's books over the years. When I went online to sign up for this workshop, there was a picture of an eagle on the Chopra website with an ad for a workshop on an Alaskan cruise. I couldn't believe that I had dreamt about needing to be with more eagles and that was one of the first things I saw on the website—a really positive sign to me that this was a good choice for me.

Meditating and Didn't Know It

Well, going to that workshop was another life-changing event for me. I learned that I had been meditating by saying my "Oms" in the shower and singing my "Praise the Lord" song to music, and I realized that I was having some of the experiences that Deepak talks about as part of the spiritual path and journey when you have a regular meditation practice. Since I had been a business major, I really had no idea whatsoever that this was what was going on with me, and at the same time I was ecstatic because I had finally found a place where I felt like I totally belonged and fit in for the first time in my life, and that was huge for me because I had felt like an ugly duckling most of my life since I was not like my mom,

Chapter Four — My Healing Really Takes Off

and she had let me know my many differences from her over and over again.

When I was at the workshop, I decided that I wanted to become a meditation teacher certified by the Chopra Center. After I got home and incorporated the new things I had learned into my daily routine, my dreams changed, and I started having "Great Mother" dreams, which I had never done before. This was really interesting to me because the "Great Mother" is considered to be the source of all life; everyone has a mother who has given them life. I had never heard of the "Great Mother" concept before that workshop. During a *namaste* exercise we did that week, all of a sudden everyone's faces turned into the faces of beautiful babies. I felt overwhelmed by all of the beautiful babies (approximately three hundred fifty people) and was very aware that very few of them realized how beautiful they really were. After my "Great Mother" dreams, I realized that all good mothers see their own babies as beautiful, and maybe God could be a woman instead of the traditional image of a white man with a beard. I went to the Seduction of Spirit workshop in November 2007, and my daughter was getting ready to start the college search process, so I decided to take the Journey into Healing required workshop on the teacher's path in November 2008 in Colorado and sign up for the teacher training then to have something to do to feel like I was making progress until I could do the actual teacher training in May 2010.

Chopra Center University

Going through that training and the preparation process before the weeklong training was really transformative for me, and when I came home to Cleveland, everyone was telling me that I was different, and my husband was looking at me really funny a lot of the time. After I finished that certification, my life took on an energy of its own, and I ended up going to three more Chopra workshops in 2010.

In January 2011, I reached a point where I realized that my hair was falling out, and I could not relax the

Chapter Four — My Healing Really Takes Off

muscles in my back even after I had three massages the week before, and I went to a hotel because I could not live in the same house with my husband anymore. I had left him a note on the kitchen table about why I left, and he emailed me and told me that he had not been happy in our marriage for a number of years (twenty-seven years, at that time), and it was probably time for us to go our separate ways. I had been praying for three years to know with perfect clarity and no regrets whether to stay or leave my marriage, and when I read that email, I thought to myself, *Well, that is pretty clear.* Then I remembered Brent Becvar telling me my life would never be the same again after October 2010 and thinking to myself, *No kidding!*

I continued my training at the Chopra Center and got certified to teach Seven Spiritual Laws of Yoga and Perfect Health/Ayurveda, which made me a vedic master. The journey through all of those trainings was incredibly healing for me and transformative in a very positive way. I loved learning in-depth about yoga and the chakras (the seven energy centers that are junction points between consciousness and the body), and I loved learning about ayurveda as well. In ayurveda, there are three main doshas (mind/body principles). Vata dosha is the wind or movement principle, pitta is the fire or transformation principle, and kapha is the earth or protection principle.

Learning about the doshas in-depth was incredibly healing because a lot of the differences between my mother and me became crystal clear to me because my dominant dosha is pitta, and my mother's dominant dosha was kapha. It made it easy to understand why she was always telling me I was bad when I didn't want the cheapest thing like she did or I didn't want to just chill all the time like she did. What was really incredible to me was that after completing all three trainings, I became aware of things in all areas of my life in a totally different way, and I became much more integrated, with my inside matching my outside much better than it ever had before. The tools and things that I have learned from this process are what have been sustaining me through a very ugly and financially hostile divorce.

Financial Abuse

I am sitting here writing this part of my book after I have just gotten a ruling for my divorce trial that ended two months ago. I am feeling total disbelief at how everything has been decided, and I cried after I read it through the first time. The way it is set up allows my ex-husband the ability to continue to financially abuse me like he has been doing for almost two years now. In spite of a healthy net worth on paper, I am living dollar to dollar right now and have been for at least a year and a half. I have lost 90 percent of the income that I was used to living on. My ex-husband has found every way possible to take little amounts of money away from me in almost every check he has given me. The ruling gives me the lowest possible amount of money from our combined assets and spreads out the amount of time for my ex to pay me to twelve years. This would prevent me from being able to pay the bills I have racked up during this process and unable to afford to sell our current home and move because my credit has been totally destroyed from being given so little money to live on during this process. Now my lawyer and I are filing objections with the judge to try to get a fairer ruling, and this will take another four to six months before we get a final decision. This will make our divorce take almost three years, and that is not including any time spent on an appeal to the judge's ruling, if there is one. I live in a small, remote suburb of Cleveland, Ohio, and my case is in Geauga County. There are only two judges in Geauga County, and neither one of them likes to deal with divorce, so they give this responsibility to a magistrate to handle. The magistrate in my case discriminates against women who do not work and/or are the plaintiffs, and this is common knowledge to everyone who has any dealings with the Geauga County Court system. Her reputation is to favor the men in those cases 100 percent and to make unfair and biased rulings for almost 100 percent of the women. I have also had many people

Chapter Four — My Healing Really Takes Off

tell me that it is not uncommon for "backdoor" deals to be made in Geauga County, especially if one of the parties has a lot of money.

When I initially met with my attorney, he thought we could be done with my divorce in as little as six months since my husband and I had been married twenty-seven years at that point, and both of my children were over eighteen years old. Yet it is two years later, and we are still not finished because my ex-husband has used every means available to him to drag this out to try to force me to accept a very small settlement from him in order for me to get this over with sooner. He is paying three attorneys to work for him, and I have one attorney. He has destroyed my credit by deliberately giving me small amounts of money before there was a support order, and then after the support order, he basically paid what he wanted to pay me, and there are no late fees or interest penalties for his not paying me the full amount on time, every time. He has bought both of my kids new cars, taken them on trips, and is even spending money on my niece and nephew (my sister's kids) to have them on "his side" and not mine because he knows I don't have much money, and he does. I learned from some of my friends that this is financial abuse, a form of domestic violence that is only just now beginning to be acknowledged and dealt with publicly. There are only a handful of states that have laws to protect against this instead of enabling the abuse to continue. It always exists where there is sexual abuse, and, as a sexual abuse survivor, I am not surprised to find out that I married someone who would financially abuse me.

In Al-Anon, we talk about the "bullfrog" effect because many of us end up "cooked" and don't even realize it until we are almost completely destroyed. The bullfrog effect means that if you put a frog in a room-temperature pot of water and turn the heat on the stove on low so that the water heats up very slowly, a little bit at a time, the frog doesn't even notice it is being boiled alive because it has grown comfortable with the very small increases in heat and temperature of the water—the frog won't even attempt to jump out of the pot. If you took a healthy frog and tried to put it in a pot of very hot water, it would quickly jump out of the pot because it is

Chapter Four — My Healing Really Takes Off

uncomfortable. I realize now that my financial devastation has really been a product of the "bullfrog" effect in my marriage because my ex-husband has been very gradually and over a long period of time taking away little bits of money from me. The end result is that now my credit has been completely destroyed, and yet this process started many years ago, and I didn't even realize what was happening at the time. The really unfortunate thing is that most states are unaware of financial abuse as something that you need to be protected from legally, and I could receive more legal protection if my ex-husband were physically beating me up right now instead of financially beating me up like he is doing.

Financial Laws Need to Change

People come up to me and tell me that they can't believe that I am going through a divorce because I look so good, and it makes me really grateful for all of my Chopra Center and other training as well as Al-Anon. I have needed all of these tools to maintain my balance as I go through this divorce. My ex-husband has plenty of money and has

I Choose Life

been able to use that to his advantage in the legal world. In spite of a court-ordered temporary support order, he has found ways to give me very little money through this process, and I have discovered a new venue on which to focus my energy going forward after my divorce is completed. I stayed home to raise my kids and did not work outside the home because I did not need to. Because my ex-husband has given me so little money, I now qualify for bankruptcy, and my credit rating has been totally destroyed. What I have learned is that this is very common in many states because of the way the divorce laws are written. There are no interest penalties or late fees for my ex-husband if he pays me late or does not pay me the full amount ordered by the court. He is able to get away with this because he owns his own business, and the attorneys let him do it because they make more money the longer this drags out.

It seems to me that if there was a change in the laws and there was a penalty for being late or interest charged on the money being paid late, a lot of this problem would go away. I'm pretty sure that my ex-husband would pay

Chapter Four — My Healing Really Takes Off

exactly what he owes on time if there were significant financial consequences for his actions. I have lost 90 percent of the income I am used to having to live on, and there is nothing I can legally do about it. I was talking to my brother about this, and he told me that in Atlanta one of the highest demands for the food banks comes from middle-class neighborhoods with women going through divorces who can't afford to feed their kids. This was really shocking to me because we are creating a really big problem down the road for the children who have grown up like this. The sadder reality to me is that I will be lucky, and financially I will be able to recover from this, but the majority of women who go through this will never be able to financially recover, and we as a collective are all paying the price for this. Every time I hear my telephone ring with a bill collector on the other end of the phone trying to get me to pay a bill that I do not have the money for, I think that all of us are paying the price for those people who make all of those phone calls. We also pay for this by having higher prices on everything to absorb the costs of accounts that have to be written off because they can't be collected. It is time for all of us to stop accepting the laws that allow this and work to get them changed to be more life-supporting for all of us.

Effects of Financial Abuse

Going through a divorce after thirty years of marriage has been very painful and educational at the same time. I have been very unaware of what was going on in the world around me financially and emotionally when families go through a divorce.

My friends at Al-Anon told me that I was and am currently being financially abused by my ex-husband. I had never heard about financial abuse before this. In a nutshell, I learned that this is when the spouse with more money withholds money deliberately to try to control the other spouse and to prevent him or her from being able to leave the marriage. Financial abuse usually includes lavishing and spending a lot of money on the children while withholding money from the other spouse so that the children are "bought" by the spouse with the most money. In many, but not all, cases, the spouse with more money is the father, and the mother is the one who gets financially abused. The ripple effect of this behavior is that the mother then has a difficult time providing for even the basic needs of food, shelter, and clothing and many times is not able to give enough of these things to her children. This compromises many children in their first chakras right away. Traditionally, mothers are the "life givers" who provide nourishment and stability for their children. We also know that scarcity causes people to shut down their emotions in the second chakra, the home of most addictions.

Addiction—The Number-One Illness

The number-one illness in the United States is addiction, and it is no surprise to me that this is happening now that I have experienced how the legal system deals with finances. There are not many ways to get money from a spouse who does not pay the full amount of support money owed or does not pay this money on time

I Choose Life

since there are no interest charges for late payments and no penalties for not paying the full amount. For most women who are owed a lot of money by ex-spouses, they do not have the money to go back to court to fight to get the money owed to them. Our system has created many mothers who do not have the financial ability to provide for the basic needs of their children, making their children prime candidates for addiction. The actions of one addict negatively affect approximately seven hundred people around them. With addiction as the number-one illness in the United States, we are all affected as one of the seven hundred people affected by addicts and their actions.

It also means that the number-one illness right now is mental illness, since addiction is classified as a mental illness. We have mental illness all around us, and it is almost impossible to avoid. We as a society are letting this happen and not doing anything to try to correct it. We all pay for the people calling to try to collect money for credit cards that can't be paid when credit has been

Chapter Four — My Healing Really Takes Off

destroyed by an ugly divorce. We all pay for the accidents and problems created by an addict not doing a good job at work. As part of Al-Anon and recovery, I learned that all addicts need to have consequences for their choices; otherwise, we are enabling them by not making them accountable for their choices. Most of our current laws do not have consequences for failure to pay on time or to pay the full court-ordered support amount.

Addiction and abuse cut across all socioeconomic barriers, and that is another reason we are all affected because there isn't really anyone exempt from this illness or the effects of this illness. When I was first talking to a publisher about my book, the woman on the other end of the phone assumed that I would go to women's shelters to talk about financial abuse with my book. I was really surprised that this was her interpretation because, throughout my divorce, I have had a number of professional women with six-figure incomes tell me how brave they think I am for leaving my marriage because of the loss of lifestyle. A lot of them have told me that they would never leave their unhappy marriages because they don't want to lose their lifestyles—and they make six-figure salaries. From my point of view, the financial abuse appears to be worse with more affluent families because the person being abused has much more to lose than someone who is used to having much less money to live on.

Everyone Is Lying

Everyone I have dealt with during my divorce—my attorney, the bankers, and other businesspeople—have all told me that they have to double check all information that I am giving them because everyone (in the general public) is lying. There is a joke in Al-Anon: "How do you know if an addict is lying? His lips are moving." This illustrates the sad truth that many alcoholics/addicts are chronic liars. This correlates to the second/fifth chakra connection: the second chakra is the seat of addiction, and the fifth chakra is blocked by lies. We are all affected by the lies of addiction in our society right now. The bigger problem here is that lies

Chapter Four — My Healing Really Takes Off

cause us to lose vital parts of our souls, and so we have a country with a large number of people who have lost many parts of their souls and are walking around lost in our society and don't know who they really are and have no idea what to do about it.

I have noticed that many people who have financial issues with their spouses will tell you that they never really talked about money and their financial values before they got married. They talked about sex and their sexual histories because of HIV, HPV, and other STDs, but they did not talk about their financial histories. Many of them have been hurt and surprised to find out that their spouses have been lying about having more money than they really do or that they were lying about not having much money when they were actually wealthy.

Sexual Abuse

The other interesting thing that I learned about financial abuse is that it is frequently present where there is sexual abuse. Sexual abuse is a first chakra issue because of the fear that comes with it and prevents the first chakra from being really strong when children grow up with a lot of fear instead of feeling safe and secure in their physical environments. After twenty-one years in Al-Anon and attending many programs about addiction, I learned that sexual abuse is present with 90 percent of addicts in treatment centers (I think it is probably closer to 100 percent, and the other 10 percent don't remember the abuse, like I did not remember it for a long time). If addiction is our number-one illness then there is a lot of financial abuse and sexual abuse going on that no one is dealing with or paying attention to.

In order to choose life, it is essential that we address these basic first chakra needs. The future wellbeing of our society depends on this since we need healthy children who are able to manage and work in our society in a healthy way once they become adults.

Teenage Suicide

One of the growing causes of death is suicide, especially with teenagers. If our first chakras are strong, and we feel really connected and nurtured by our families and the communities around us, then we want to live

Chapter Four — My Healing Really Takes Off

because we feel strong and safe in the world. If we have lived with a lot of deprivation because our first chakra needs haven't been met and have witnessed our parents treating each other very poorly and spouses not providing enough money for even basic needs to be met then we start to feel hopeless about our future in the world. Our children are the future of the world, and if a large number of them are killing themselves, what kind of a future are we creating?

Getting grounded is the essential first step to healing and transforming our lives. We need to work on this personally and as a society to help deal with the addiction all around us that affects us whether we think so or not. "The world will not be destroyed by those who do evil but by those who watch them without doing anything" (Albert Einstein). We have the power to work together to bring about change that supports life instead of destroys it.

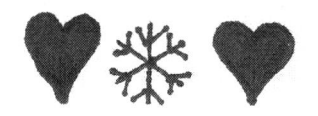

Chapter Five — Consciously Choosing Life

The Guest House by Rumi(24)

This being human is a guest house.

Every morning a new arrival.

A joy, a depression, a meanness,

some momentary awareness comes

as an unexpected visitor.

Welcome and entertain them all.

Even if they are a crow of sorrows,

who violently sweep your house

empty of its furniture,

still, treat each guest honorably.

He may be clearing you out

for some new delight.

The dark thought, the shame, the malice,

meet them at the door laughing,

and invite them in.

Be grateful for whoever comes,

because each has been sent

as a guide from beyond.

Choosing Life

"Now choose life" (Deuteronomy 30:19). "You will show me the path of life" (Psalm 16:11). We are instructed to choose life in the scriptures and trust that God or the universe will show us the path of life when this is our intention. Choosing life starts in the first chakra by getting really strong in our roots and taking good care of our basic survival needs and having good self-care.

Chapter Five — Consciously Choosing Life

In Al-Anon, one of the first things we learn is to start talking to other people and reaching out to them for support; this strengthens our first chakras by giving us a community where we belong and feel supported. We also start to learn about being more aware of the choices we are making and how they will affect us, and the others around us.

We have the ability with every choice we make throughout the day to consciously choose life. Even having the intention of wanting to always choose life will help us to be supported by the universe in every choice we make.

I Choose Life

Diagram of chakra locations within the body

Chapter Five — Consciously Choosing Life

Working with My Chakras

Recently all of these many pieces of my journey have all come together in a meaningful way about how we can find a way to be more authentic and get in touch with our dharmas or life/soul's purposes, and it starts with the chakras in our bodies. Everyone has seven main chakras (energy centers), and they are commonly known as: first chakra, root chakra, muladhara chakra (color is red); second chakra, creativity/sexuality chakra, svadisthana chakra (color is orange); third chakra, solar plexus chakra, manipura chakra (color is yellow); fourth chakra, heart chakra, anahata chakra (color is green); fifth chakra, throat chakra, vishuddha chakra (color is sky blue); sixth chakra, third-eye chakra, ajna chakra (color is indigo blue); and seventh chakra, crown chakra, sahaswara chakra (color is violet, or white in some traditions). Each of these chakras has attributes and characteristics, as well as vibrations, associated with it. All of the chakras have yoga poses that help strengthen and restore them. It is important to maintain balance in each of the chakras, because too much energy in one direction or the other will usually cause problems; these problems may result in our being *out of balance* and needing to look for remedies to restore balance to our bodies and lives. In ayurveda people with serious illnesses are considered to be drastically out of balance; the idea is that better or improved health starts to return when balance starts to get restored.

First Chakra

Energy comes into our bodies through our feet then up our legs and into the first chakra. All of this area of the body—the feet, legs, and base of the spine—is a part of the first chakra energy. This chakra is associated with being a victim or being fully nourished and also with our sense of belonging and safety in our families, communities, and the world. Part of being nourished besides food is to feel fully and completely safe and to have enough money or resources to provide for our basic needs in life: food, shelter, and clothing. If we do not have a lot of energy flowing through this chakra then the other

Chapter Five — Consciously Choosing Life

six chakras are compromised because there is less and less energy available to them as the energy moves from our feet up to the top of our heads. I heard Brene Brown speaking on "Oprah" recently, and she said that when there is scarcity or not enough for your basic needs to be met then the emotions shut down, and two things that everyone needs are a sense of belonging and a feeling of being worthy of being loved. For women going through financial stress, like I am, during a divorce, this prevents us from being able to provide for the basic (first chakra) needs of our children, therefore shutting down the children's emotions. It can also lead to women leaving their children with "free" or "sketchy" babysitters because they do not have the money to pay for appropriate childcare. Unfortunately, because Mom has become financially desperate, it puts her children at a higher risk for poor supervision, leaving the door open for injuries and/or abuse, both physical and sexual.

The first chakra is also the one associated with "grounding" and giving strength to the rest of the system to survive. Grounding activities are anything that involves physical exercise or movement, like dancing, and anything that requires physical labor, like cutting the grass or labor inside the house, like chopping up vegetables or ironing clothes. This is why those in monasteries have known for a long time that if one of the nuns has a big spiritual experience, they send her to the kitchen to peel potatoes for three hours to get her grounded and completely back into her body. On some military bases, anyone who has gotten disciplined is also sent to the kitchen to peel potatoes to help him calm down from whatever has happened and get him completely back into his body. The grounding is vitally important; the first chakra is called the root chakra because of the importance of having "roots" firmly planted in the ground. Any living tree or plant cannot grow to its full beauty and size without its roots being stable and firmly planted in the ground. Our roots need to be capable of supporting the growth we want to experience in our lives, and if we spend too much time on the upper chakras and very little on the first

Chapter Five — Consciously Choosing Life

chakra then our tree falls over (which is what happened to me when I blew out my kundalini) or dies because it does not have enough support and energy to handle the extra load placed on it.

The first chakra and being grounded is also what gives us patience and endurance to hang in there instead of looking for the quickest "fix" possible. Incredible structures like the Sistine Chapel and the Egyptian pyramids required years and years of work to be completed—which is what being grounded is all about. I learned recently that it took Thomas Edison almost forty years to develop a light bulb that worked. Close to the time of his successful light bulb, he wrote down that he had discovered ten thousand ways that didn't work. I never thought of it that way, but this is an example of incredible groundedness to me.

The first chakra is where we get our sense of belonging, and it is essential to our survival to feel like we really belong somewhere. Over the years in Al-Anon, I have heard many speakers talk about how they never really felt like they belonged anywhere or really fit in and how difficult this was for them. When I feel like I belong somewhere, it means that I feel safe there, and safety is really the primary need to be met in the first chakra because if we don't feel safe then we start making choices out of fear and as a victim instead of from a place of being strong and healthy. After the last incident when I was ten years old, I put on a lot of weight, and I have heard a lot of adult women say they don't dress attractively or work on their weight issues because then men will leave them alone; this is a common experience for survivors of sexual abuse.

Part of belonging is being active and involved in a community that supports you. Many years ago, this need for community support was often met by religious institutions, and I have had a number of people tell me that the nuns were the best because they gave them encouragement and nourishment that made up for things they did not get at home. It would have helped me to feel like I had a community of support instead of

Chapter Five — Consciously Choosing Life

being totally and completely dependent on my mother when I was growing up. This community of support is a part of having our roots firmly planted in the ground and knowing that we have many people who could help or support us when we need it if our parents are not available to help us. Another reason a community of support is important is because "environment is stronger than will" (Paramahansa Yogananda).(25) The people we associate with become part of our environment, and they can have a positive or negative effect on us. It is important to be able to associate with people who make you feel safe: "Choose carefully the people you associate with" (Paramahansa Yogananda taught this to remind us that the vibrations of the people around us are important).(26)

I also feel like I belong when I am with other people who are like me. In the career-planning class I took right out of college, the teacher told us that people in each category of jobs are all like each other, and she told us to start looking for the people who are like us, and we would know where we belonged. After the first "Project Runway" (27) television program, my daughter told me a number of times that I was just like Austin on the show. It is interesting to me that "Project Runway" is a show for fashion designers, and when I was five years old, I had drawn dress designs that weren't understood by my mother. My childhood instincts about who I was were good but never got developed because my mother did not understand at all how to help me to grow and develop my innate talents. This is also why I felt like I instantly belonged when I got to the Chopra Center because I am here to walk a spiritual path, and spirituality is one of the core teachings at the Chopra Center.

Some other important things associated with the first chakra are the ability to flow and be flexible. Points of constriction in our physical bodies are usually what eventually lead to physical diseases manifesting in our bodies. The ability to continually stay flexible and flow with the changing events around us comes from the first chakra, and being well grounded is essential to being able

Chapter Five — Consciously Choosing Life

to do this easily. Being grounded gives us the ability to be patient with people and circumstances when things are not instantly the way we want them to be. Some other basic needs of healthy eating and nourishing food are associated with the first chakra. I have heard many AA talks about how the speakers sometimes went without dinner or food for a whole day because their mothers didn't fix food or have the money to buy them food.

One of the most important things to strengthen your first chakra is to get a good night's sleep on a consistent basis as well as having some times of rest during the day. We are a country of sleep-deprived people, and sleeping problems are among the most common health problems in the United States. Many busy people will cut out sleep in order to get it all done, and this ends up impacting their physical health because our bodies need adequate sleep and rest in order to maintain good health and balance. This has been one of the biggest changes that I have made over the years, and it has made a very big difference in my overall health and wellbeing. Another factor contributing to sleeping problems is excessive anxiety and worrying. Collectively, we all took a big hit in increased anxiety after the September 11, 2001, terrorist attack. The issues of anxiety and worry become less of a problem with regular exercise, becoming more aware of your body, and knowing when your body needs to rest or sleep a little more. It is really difficult to be in tune with your body and what is going on with it unless you are really well grounded and are taking care of your body's basic needs consistently.

Other first chakra needs are basic things like good hygiene and clean clothes. I have heard Al-Anon members' stories about how no one ever supervised them, taking care of brushing their teeth or bathing on a regular basis. Many adults who did not learn how to take care of their clothes and basic appearance growing up have no idea how to take care of these things now because they did not learn about them when they were younger. I had to work on paying more attention to my daily hygiene and only buying clothes that really fit me instead of making due with something the

Chapter Five — Consciously Choosing Life

wrong size because it was cheaper (which was something my kapha –people who generally don't like to spend a lot of money or buy the cheapest thing–mother imposed on me because, from her point of view, cheaper was always better). When there is not adequate grounding, these needs do not get taken care of on a consistent basis, and consistency is essential to maintaining good health and balance.

For those of us who have been victims of either physical or sexual abuse, it is essential to focus on strengthening the first chakra for several reasons. Without working on strengthening the first chakra, the victim becomes the victimizer of other people around them. It takes conscious and consistent effort to strengthen your first chakra to start healing the "victim" within you and establish new habits that are really nourishing and healthy for you. People with serious illnesses like cancer or AIDS are not able to hold much energy in their first chakras, and in order to really heal their bodies, they need to focus on strengthening their first chakras and allowing more energy to enter their entire chakra system.

I Choose Life

In many of Mother Teresa's books, she talks about how the worst disease is to be not wanted, and it dawned on me that this is because if we don't feel wanted then we do not feel like we belong. My grandmother was in her thirties when she had my mother, and, in those days, that was viewed as a bad thing and was not commonly accepted like it is today. My mother told me that my grandmother made comments all the time about how embarrassing it was for her to have a small child at her age. My mother was four months pregnant with Anne when my dad died, and she told Anne that it was too late for her to have an abortion then. Anne told me a number of times how upsetting this was for her to hear because her own mother had never wanted her, and Anne really believed this.

In the Seven Spiritual Laws of Yoga taught by the Chopra Center (located in Carlsbad, CA; www.chopra.com) (28), the first chakra is associated with the law of karma or cause and effect. This is the chakra where it is really important to make the most nourishing choices

Chapter Five — Consciously Choosing Life

instead of making a lot of toxic choices, which will compromise the flow of energy for the rest of the chakra system.

The most work that I have done on myself over twenty-one years of recovery has been on strengthening my first chakra because of the safety violations that I went through in my childhood. Because I didn't feel safe, I wanted to die instead of continuing to live around my stepfather, who was absolutely not safe from my point of view. Even though I did a lot of other work that definitely helped me feel better along the way, it was not until I was able to completely remember the entire incident when I was nine years old that I could know with certainty within myself that I now wanted to live because I have a purpose of helping others feel better and also because now I'm not afraid to write about my story and tell the truth. Until I remembered this feeling from long ago, it was a part of my energy system and influenced all of my choices, whether I was aware of it or not. By remembering this feeling and working on healing this feeling within me, I was able to make healthier choices for myself independently of this energy that had been a part of me for a very long time.

Everything else with our chakra systems depend on the strength of our first chakras, and if you only have a few minutes a day to work on yourself, doing something to strengthen the first chakra is the most essential thing to start with.

Second Chakra

The second chakra is located below the belly button and above the root chakra. This chakra is the seat of our emotions, our creative/sexual energy, and the home of our authentic selves. The color associated with this chakra is orange so it is not too surprising that I, a sexual abuse survivor who had not been allowed to explore my creativity, had no orange in my life. If the needs of the first chakra are not adequately met then the second chakra does not have a very strong flow of energy and compromises us in all of these areas associated with the second chakra. The

Chapter Five — Consciously Choosing Life

second chakra is associated with pleasure in life and how much or how little pleasure we allow ourselves to have or not have; it also has the on/off switch for your appetite. In addition to being the home of our authentic selves, the second chakra is associated with addiction because there are either too many blockages here, or there is not a strong enough energy flow going through here, or both. Guilt is what blocks the second chakra, and we can carry guilt because we have "too much" pleasure or because we don't sacrifice enough to help others or because we want something that is in conflict with our families or their values, and they don't approve of how much pleasure we wanted or allowed ourselves to have or not have. When we have grown up hearing "no," "stop it," or "don't do that" a lot of the time, there is automatic guilt if we engage in any of these "forbidden" activities.

When the second chakra is blocked, we feel disconnected from our senses and our bodies. After about five years in Al-Anon, I remember thinking something was wrong with my arms and legs. I asked an energy counselor about this, and she smiled and laughed a little. She said there was nothing wrong with me; I was just physically starting to have and be aware of feelings in my arms and legs for the first time because I had been shut down a long time ago, and now they were coming alive again as I was healing. I did not even know that I wasn't really connected to my body and feeling all of it until this happened. I had a regular exercise routine by then, which was strengthening my first chakra and making me feel more alive in my body than I had ever been before.

The second chakra is where we are able to relate to others with ease and how we make connections with others. What happens with addiction is that the addict has an emotional relationship with a thing instead of other people, which is not what our emotions were designed for. Anyone who has had a parent die before the age of seven has a hole in their second chakra because of the impact of the loss of the parent at such a young age. Fifty percent of adults who experience the death of a parent when they were children end up becoming addicted. The issue

Chapter Five — Consciously Choosing Life

of sexual abuse comes up again in this chakra because many victims are made to feel guilty that this happened to them, as if the abuse were somehow their fault, and guilt blocks the second chakra.

As I was learning about reiki and exercising more, I started cleaning up areas of clutter around my house. The second chakra is connected to having order in our lives instead of a lot of chaos or turbulence. I have heard some people describe chaos as "too much drama," and all of these terms are referring to how much order we have in our lives. I liked it when I realized that by cleaning up the clutter as I was healing, I was adding more order into my life instead of the clutter and drama I had grown up with as "normal."

It is almost impossible to be your authentic self if the issues of your second chakra are not dealt with. Being our authentic selves is what helps us to be able to look for and find other people who are like us, so we know where we belong and fit in. For people who do not remember what happened to them, working with your dreams is a way to start finding pieces of yourself or having repressed memories triggered from something that was in a dream. I have witnessed amazing healing for people working with the energy in their dreams and realizing what happened when they were children but can now do something to change it or heal it as adults. It helped me to get more grounded and learn to "listen" to my body, as we learn in yoga, and then I could also decide if something was an emotionally good choice for me or not. (Many people with serious illnesses have trouble holding much energy in the second chakra.)

I also started learning about my authentic self by looking at how I spent my money and what I would give away or let go of instead when I had to cut back on my spending. The things we spend our money on give us clues about who our authentic selves really are and what our values are.

There are seven billion people on Planet Earth, and no two have the same fingerprints; this is amazing to me. It is hard for me to get my mind around seven billion different choices of anything. We were not created to be the same, and a lot of my "don't do that" and "you're bad" messages came because of my being different than my family of origin. It has been really healing for me to embrace my uniqueness and to focus on the "fingerprint" or piece of Divine love that I am here to contribute to the world. Even though we are created uniquely, something we have in common is emotional experiences that feel the same. So at the level of our emotions, this is where we can connect with other people by identifying and talking about the common feelings and emotional experiences we have had in our lives. This is difficult to do if the second chakra is blocked or shut down.

Third Chakra

The third chakra is associated with our self-esteem and our feelings of worthiness or being "good enough." This is the chakra associated with our ability to manifest and have power in the world, and it is the home of the hidden treasures within our beings. Shame blocks our third chakra, and any time we receive the message that we are bad, it affects this chakra and our belief in our own power in the world and many times can cause us to give our power away to others because we don't feel good enough to stand in our own unique power. Shame gives us a lot of fear of our connections being broken, which makes many of those with big shame issues do things for other people out of fear of losing the relationship instead of doing them because they want to.

This is where we have our desires, and it is where we get our energy and vitality to accomplish things. There is a Bible verse, Psalm 37:4, "Delight yourself in the Lord and he will give you the desires of your heart." In order to have this happen, we need to know what we want, and this is almost impossible if we have been made to feel guilty about what we wanted. Deepak tells us that if we don't know what we want, we are going nowhere because our desires are like the rudder on a ship and give us direction in life. Even if you want to dedicate yourself to helping the poor and needy, that is still a "want." It is okay

Chapter Five — Consciously Choosing Life

to have wants and desires, and having them gives us our direction in life. I did not have a lot of direction in my life until I had healed some of my third chakra issues and started getting in touch with what my real desires were. Right after I wrote this, there was a post on Facebook: "To cultivate joy, pay attention to what you like" (from *The Afterlife of Billy Fingers*).(29)

When I started going to Al-Anon, I had no idea what I wanted; I could only tell you what other people wanted because I had been made to feel guilty and labeled "bad" for the pitta things I wanted that conflicted with the kapha things my mother wanted when I was growing up. Because I didn't know what I wanted, I gave a lot of my power away to other people and let them make decisions and choices for me. I had to start with really little things like buying clothes I liked or doing something nice for myself like a massage or manicure to start to explore and learn what I even liked.

The third chakra is the home of the "hidden jewel" within us. There is a Rumi quote: "Why are you looking for treasure outside yourself when the real treasure house is within you?" (30) The third chakra is where this real treasure lives in our bodies and energy systems. I started learning and connecting with many treasures within myself when I started working with my dreams and learning about the archetypes and animals that showed up in my dreams over and over again on a consistent basis. I started making conscious efforts to honor what showed up in my dreams by doing research or reading a book or watching a movie about something from one of my dreams. This made my life a lot more interesting, and I have not been bored in a really long time. One of the things I have had many people tell me is that I am a really interesting person, and a lot of that has come from embracing the "jewels" that have come to me from my dreams. The other really neat thing from working with my dreams on a regular basis is that I have more and more synchronicities showing up around me as I connect more of my insides with my outsides.

"Any form of art is a form of power" (Ossie Davis). (31) This became a really important quote for me because

Chapter Five — Consciously Choosing Life

I had wanted to take art classes when I was growing up, and my mother wouldn't let me. So I started taking art classes, and then the Artist's Way class opened up a whole new world for me and gave me a way to get in touch with my power and to start taking my power back that I had given away to other people. This did not always go well because other people, especially my ex-husband, liked having power over me. He didn't really like it at all that I was taking back my own power and not letting him make all of the choices for me anymore. Yet I knew that if I didn't take my power back, I was going nowhere for the rest of my life. Connecting with art and nurturing my creative skills by making art quilts was reconnecting me with having beauty in my life and giving me a creative outlet for honoring my dreams and experiences. I like things to be pretty, and my mother would make me feel guilty because the pretty things were generally more expensive than the ordinary things that she liked, and she would tell me that I was being selfish to want something so expensive. Developing my art skills gave me a way to have pretty things around me in a more affordable way and also gave me my own unique power and way of expressing myself.

Fourth Chakra

The fourth chakra is also known as our heart chakra and is located in the middle of your chest. This is the chakra associated with giving and receiving love as well as having hope, empathy, and compassion for others. The heart chakra can be blocked by: sadness, resentments, grievances, or regrets. The Egyptians had a belief that you'd want your heart to be as light as a feather at the time of your death—to be lighthearted. The heart is figuratively and literally in the middle of everything since it is between the first three chakras associated with our physical bodies and the last three chakras associated with our spiritual development and connection to spirit. The heart chakra is the literal "balance point" of the seven chakras in our bodies and the most important one to work on when you need to restore more balance

Chapter Five — Consciously Choosing Life

in your life. In energy medicine, the heart chakra contains all seven chakras within it, and, ideally speaking, you can heal anything through the heart chakra because of this. The heart chakra is the balance point between heaven and earth in our bodies. The heart radiates an electromagnetic field that affects others' moods, attitudes, and feelings, whether we are conscious of it or not (Institute of Heartmath). (32) I heard Marilyn Schlitz of the Institute of Noetic Sciences (33) talk about research that confirms this and how much we are affected by the emotions of the people who live in the same house with us—especially the emotions they feel toward us, either positive or negative.

I have a friend who graduated from Cornell, and she played goalie for their soccer team. She told me that she got hit really hard in the head with a soccer ball once; she was not able to speak, but she could hear and see what was going on around her as people were trying to help her. She told me that she could see the feelings coming out of each person's hearts toward her, and she was surprised to learn that some people she didn't think cared very much about her were really concerned about her being hurt. She said it was also surprising to her that some of the people whom she thought were her good friends were not as concerned about her wellbeing. She now has five children, and she works on remembering this when she is having an issue with her children because she doesn't want them to think that she doesn't love them even if she is correcting them for something they have done.

In Chinese medicine, the heart is considered the "brain" (or the "mind") of the body because the heart, and the condition of our heart chakras, really determines the final choices we make or don't make. The heart chakra is located where our hearts and lungs are located, and we cannot live without a heartbeat or our breath. We can start to clear and open up blockages in this chakra by starting to work with our breath—a fundamental part of yoga called pranayama and something that many people in the Western world are out of touch with. We have an expression about this: "the breath of life." And in the Bible

Chapter Five — Consciously Choosing Life

it says: "God breathed the breath of life into his nostrils" (Genesis 2:7). There is another quote: "All things share the same breath—the beast, the tree, the man. The air shares its spirit with all the life it supports" (Chief Seattle).(34)

Some more interesting information from the Institute of Heartmath is that your heart emits electromagnetic fields that change according to your emotions, and the human heart's magnetic field can be measured up to several feet away from the body. (35) This is how we affect the people around us, especially the people living in the same house with us. When you have spent a lot of hours in meditation, this electromagnetic field around you gets larger and larger, and I have heard that some yogis with advanced meditation and yoga practices can affect an area of up to a thousand-mile radius around them just because of the energy field and vibrations they have built around themselves through regular meditation and yoga practice.

The fourth chakra is the home of our soul's purpose, or dharma in Sanskrit. If we have experienced a lot of trauma, loss, or sadness then we can lose parts of our soul, and it is unclear to us what our soul's purpose is, and we feel lost in the world around us. I like this explanation of soul loss from Robert Moss in his book *The Three Only Things*: "We lose soul when we make the choice to give up on our big dreams, when we refuse to make that creative leap of faith, or to trust ourselves to love. We lose soul when we take up the habit of lying to ourselves or to others. Our dreams show us how to heal our divided selves and bring missing parts of our energy identity back into the body, where they belong." (36) These are the pieces that I have been gathering since my breakthrough so that I can put my picture together and see what my soul purpose looks like that has been missing from my energy for a long time. This has felt like I am putting together a puzzle with a thousand pieces in it, and the middle pieces have been missing, so I haven't been able to know what the complete picture looks like.

Even though I have been working on parts of this book for seven years, I have been afraid to put my whole story in writing to share with the world until I remembered the

Chapter Five — Consciously Choosing Life

last piece of the memory that happened when I was nine years old. I know that seeing that knife at my mother's throat made me feel totally hopeless because life would not be worth living if there wasn't anyone who really loved me like my mother did, and there would have been no way for me to not tell about the knife to others once I remembered it. The length of the process of remembering all my missing pieces that happened to me is a very clear example of why a strong first chakra is essential; I would not have had the energy to stick with this unless I had strengthened my first chakra.

"The awakened heart is a lamp" (Rumi).(37) I believe that going to Al-Anon and practicing my "praise the Lord" mantra woke my heart up and helped me to find the next right step and the next right thing to do as I have been working on healing from my childhood traumas. This is another reason that it is important to work on recovering the parts of your soul that you have lost so that you can find your way and not feel lost anymore.

"For where your treasure is, there will your heart be also" (Matthew 6:21). This verse turned out to be completely true for me and helped me to really learn what my values are and what the priorities in my heart were when I started looking at where I spent my money and what was worth it to me or not. During the time my kids were growing up, I spent most of my money on them and their activities because I wanted them to be able to discover their talents and abilities while they were still growing up instead of having to go on a big search for them like I have had to do as an adult since my breakthrough. (Yet the yogis would say that everything is as it should be, so this is the way my path is and was supposed to be unfolding.) More recently, I have spent most of my money on developing my skills and interests and getting certified as a teacher through Chopra Center University.

"The Gentiles are darkened in their understanding and separated from the life of God because of the ignorance that is in them due to the hardening of their hearts" (Ephesians 4:18). This verse teaches us that having "hard hearts" or blocked heart chakras causes us to make ignorant choices for ourselves and to be separated from God

Chapter Five — Consciously Choosing Life

because when we have too many blockages in our heart chakras, we are afraid to trust others and let ourselves be vulnerable about how we really feel. This adversely affects our relationships with others because we can't have real intimacy with others unless we allow ourselves to be really honest about our feelings, making ourselves vulnerable to others and their reactions or responses to us. This chakra also contributes to misunderstandings when people say one thing and then do something else, or they are not completely honest about how they feel, which can cause misunderstandings down the road in their relationships.

"Love is the dance of your life. Hence those who do not know what love is have missed the very dance of life" (Osho). (38) If we don't allow ourselves to be vulnerable, we miss out on experiencing real love and participating in the dance of life. I have a friend whose husband tells their kids that life is not a spectator sport, and they need to be in the "game" of life. When I started going to Al-Anon, I was barely participating in the game of life because I had given away a lot of my power to others, and I was afraid to let anyone see that I wasn't perfect or to even try new things because I was afraid that they wouldn't work out or that I wouldn't be good at them. Playing it safe all the time kept me on the sidelines as a spectator, watching other people play the "game" of life. I am not a spectator anymore, and writing this book is taking a huge step at letting myself be vulnerable and to really participate in the game of life.

Sometime in the first two years of Al-Anon, I started to realize that people were trying to be nice to me, and I was keeping them away and not letting them in to see who I really was. I started praying every day for God to help me to let people into my life who were sincere and really trying to help me instead of keeping all of them at safe distance away from the real me. There is a Rumi quote about looking for the barriers within ourselves that we have built up to keep love out, and without even knowing who Rumi was, this is what I had started to do when I started praying to be able to let other people into

Chapter Five — Consciously Choosing Life

my life and let them see who I really am. (39) It has taken a lot of effort for me to clear out enough of the barriers so that I could let myself be vulnerable and take a chance that other people would not hurt me as deeply as my stepfather had done when I was growing up. I had a lot of sadness that I needed to heal in order to help me accomplish this.

The physical sensation associated with the heart chakra is touch, and when I learned about this, I realized that my mother had a lot of emotional intelligence when she rocked with me on her lap after my stepfather had raped me. Being on her lap and rocking back and forth helped me reconnect with her physical body by touching her and also because I could feel her love for me while we rocked in the rocking chair. My mother was also giving me her undivided attention, which is another need of the heart. We all need attention, and some people will go to really drastic lengths to get their need for attention met. My grandfather told me many, many times that I had his undivided attention, and over the years I have appreciated this more and more as time goes by, especially when I see families sitting at tables in restaurants and all four people are doing something with their smartphones or playing video games and giving a very poor quality of attention to each other. I heard a healer once say that the really sad thing is that some people are willing to die in order to get a huge amount of attention (even if it is for a short time) and that he has seen this in some cancer patients he worked with, and they didn't care if they were dying from cancer because they were receiving the most attention they had ever received in their lives. I went through a lot of healing when I started learning to give this quality of attention to myself and to pay attention to what was going on with me first before making choices about how to spend my time and energy.

Neglect is one of the hardest things to heal energetically because it deprives the heart of two things it really needs: touch (affection) and attention. People who have been neglected will often trust dangerous people just because they are showing them attention and/or

Chapter Five — Consciously Choosing Life

affection, which is something they did not get enough of while growing up. Neglect makes people very compliant with others because they literally don't know better. I often wonder who is touching our children when Mom and Dad are both working full time, and I wonder if this doesn't leave some of these children at risk for sexual abuse because they like the touching and attention.

There has been fascinating research done by Masaru Emoto (40) on the effects of meditation and positive words like "love" and the effects the words have on water crystals placed in a bowl. The water in a bowl with the label "love" on it forms water crystals that look like perfect snowflakes, and the water in a bowl with the word "hate" on it are not cohesive or well-formed at all, and many of them are ugly and unattractive. It is amazing to me how the difference in a single word can make such a big difference in a bowl of water, especially since our bodies are made up mostly of water (approximately 80 percent of our bodies are made up of water). What are we doing to our bodies if we don't love them exactly the way they are and feel grateful for what we do have? When I learned about this research, I was really glad for the positive affirmations I had started incorporating into my daily routine because now I know that those positive affirmations have helped me heal my body and emotions. Learning to love myself and my body more gave me the ability to give more love to others very easily. This is one of the areas of myself that I have worked on the hardest, and now all of that effort is totally worth it to me.

I included two pictures of the research results by Masaru Emoto and a picture showing how much the specific parts of our bodies are made up of water. It is very clear to me that the words I use when I talk to myself directly affect the health of the rest of my body.

Chapter Five — Consciously Choosing Life

Masaru Emoto – Emoto Peace Project

The text in this picture reads as follows:

A bowl containing mineral water (arrows) was placed on the table in front of Dadi Janki administrative head of Brahma Kumaris World Spiritual University during a morning meditation on October 10, 2009. Water crystal photographs were taken from the mineral water before/after meditation.

I Choose Life

Pictures of Water and How It Is Affected by Our Words

Chapter Five — Consciously Choosing Life

THE HUMAN BODY

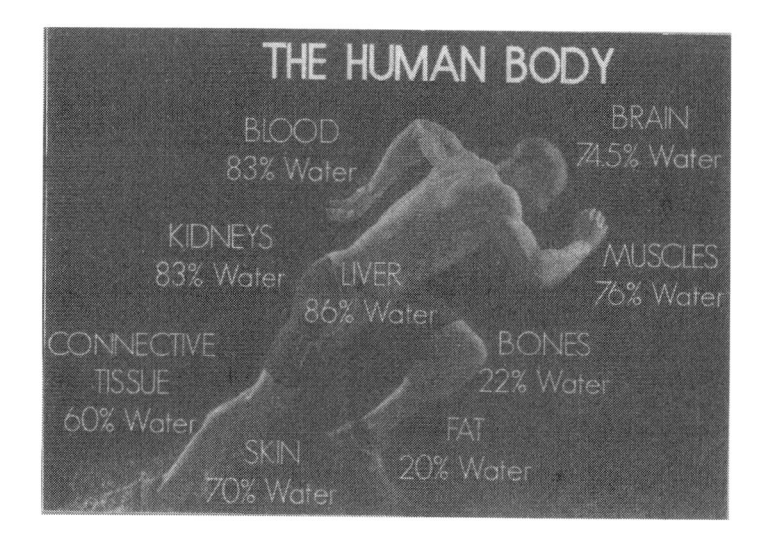

BLOOD 83% Water
BRAIN 74.5% Water
KIDNEYS 83% Water
LIVER 86% Water
MUSCLES 76% Water
CONNECTIVE TISSUE 60% Water
BONES 22% Water
SKIN 70% Water
FAT 20% Water

Water in the Human Body

Fifth Chakra

The fifth chakra is located in our throats, and it is associated with how we communicate in the world. It is connected with the message we want to send and communicate to others, and it is very often where we give ourselves permission to do something different or send a new message or write a "new story" instead of the painful or sad story we grew up with. The throat chakra is connected to healing because our words can be uplifting to others, especially when we use the word "love" because the vibration from that word is very powerful at restoring order and correcting chaos. "The tongue has the power of life and death" (Proverbs 18:21); this is especially true since our throat chakra is where we tell the truth or lies, either to others or to ourselves. The throat chakra is blocked by lies, and in order to start clearing the blockage here, it is important to start telling the truth to other people and to ourselves. Lying causes soul loss and affects us and other people around us more than we realize.

As I have gone through my divorce, I have been really surprised by how many people do not believe what I am

Chapter Five — Consciously Choosing Life

telling them unless I can prove it to them. I have learned that most of the population is lying about something, and that is why banks and lawyers are so skeptical if you are telling the truth unless you can prove it. I have thought about it many times when my phone rings with someone trying to collect money from me and I don't have it because of my divorce; we, as a country, are all paying for this because of the lies that are causing the need for more bill collectors and loans being written off. The money to pay for this gets added into everything we buy and makes it so that all of us are paying for this behavior.

Our throat chakra is what we use to tell our "message" to the world and communicate our needs and wants to others. Our personal messages we send out to others also get communicated to those around us by the way we live and the way we dress ourselves. It is important to be aware of the message we want to send to others and to make sure that the message we send is the one we wanted to send. When I was teaching art at vacation Bible school one year, I heard one of the children say that you know someone loves you when your name is safe in their mouth. I have never forgotten this because this is part of the message that we send to others whether we realize it or not.

This is where a lot of purification takes place for many people on a spiritual path because they learn more effective and pleasant ways to get their messages across than they used to. One of the first things I remember learning in Al-Anon was that it was important to "say what I mean, mean what I say, but don't say it mean." This was a totally new concept for me and before I learned about this, I would say what I meant in very mean ways because that was what I learned in my dysfunctional family when I was growing up. I also used to say yes to things when I really wanted to say no, but I was afraid of not pleasing someone else or because I had given my power to someone else and I did what they were telling me to do even though I really didn't want to do what they were telling me to do. This was a huge change for me when I started to say no when I wanted to and to tell the truth about

Chapter Five — Consciously Choosing Life

why I felt that way. This is important because then we are being totally reliable about taking care of ourselves while also being honest with the other people in our lives. It is really damaging for children to live in a household where the truth is not spoken most of the time because it erodes their ability to trust what other people tell them. It can also lead to the child's developing a very cynical viewpoint as it becomes very obvious that people just say things to be polite but then don't really mean them or keep their words.

This is also where we learn to speak up because, as I have heard Deepak say a number of times, "If you don't say anything, the problem gets worse." This is especially true when dealing with addiction. If we don't speak up and address problems with our children out of fear of losing them to the other parent then the addiction problem will just get worse. Even though these are not always pleasant conversations, they are necessary because energy and the vibration of "love" always correct chaos. Speaking up and correcting our children or other people in our lives who are creating problems for us makes them healthier, as well as the family and community around them.

The throat chakra is also affected by keeping secrets that we don't tell other people because we are afraid of getting in trouble, being rejected or losing a connection with someone we care about. In Al-Anon, I learned that it is common knowledge that we are as "sick as our secrets." In order to make progress in recovery and healing, it is important to start exposing our secrets and being honest about things we know or that we have done. In alcoholic families, one of the biggest problems is that they don't communicate very well with each other, and a lot of this is because of secrets that aren't being told and also because the family hasn't learned better communication skills or what healthy communication is. Habits such as gossiping or criticism come from an imbalance in the throat chakra and these habits usually start to fall away or disappear as we strengthen and balance our throat chakras.

Singing or chanting or reading out loud are all things that help strengthen our throat chakras and allow us to

Chapter Five — Consciously Choosing Life

get more comfortable sharing our voices with the world around us. "Be your note" (Rumi). This makes me think of the throat chakra and how we all have a "note" to play in the bigger symphony of life, and in order to share our note with the world, we need to have strong throat chakras that allow us to share our message with the world and the people around us. Sound is one of the best ways to release stress from our physical bodies. I think this is why people have a tendency to yell when they get upset because they feel better after they yell, although this usually doesn't have a very good result in the long run. Chakra toning is a form of chanting, as well as saying mantras with sun salutations. Both of these activities are good things to help release stress from your physical body.

"Holding forth the word of life" (Philippians 2:16). Our words have the power to give life or death to others. I think we all know people who use their words like bullets and how painful it is to be on the receiving end of those bullets. I heard someone recently say that someone's words were like poison to them, and this is also a very painful position to be in. My grandfather lifted me up many times with his kind words to me, and his words were life-giving to me. As Dr. Maya Angelou says, "People will forget what you said, people will forget what you did, but people will never forget how you made them feel." (41) Our words play an important part in how we make other people feel. I believe that using our words to give life to others is a way to be "God's kiss" to others to help lift them up and feel supported whenever possible.

"Let every thing that hath breath praise the Lord" (Psalm 150:6). This verse encourages us to use our voices to praise the Lord, express gratitude for the gifts all around us, and to be grateful for what we have. If we have filled our hearts with gratitude, it is easy to offer praise and gratitude to others. When I first came to Al-Anon, this was a totally crazy thought to me, and I couldn't believe that I was supposed to be grateful when I had such "serious" problems to deal with in my life. I have had to work on this over and over and over again to get myself to the point where it comes naturally to me. Going through my divorce and losing 90 percent of my normal income brought me back to the beginning again and having to work on being grateful for what I still have, including my warm bed to sleep in, a washing machine, and a car that works and gets me to the places I want and need to go.

Sixth Chakra

The sixth chakra is located in the middle of our foreheads in between our eyebrows, and it is quite literally connected with our brains, the quality of our thoughts, and also our insights and intuition, and is commonly referred to as the third-eye chakra. Many people in Al-Anon and AA talk about "stinking thinking," and I didn't know it when I went to Al-Anon in the beginning, but I had really stinking thinking and had no awareness at all of the effects that my thinking was having on my day-to-day life and the experiences that I was having in the world.

By now, I hope you are starting to see the strong connection between having a lot of good energy coming into our first chakras because we still want a good flow of energy by the time it gets to our brains so we can use our brains to think of good choices for ourselves. Since our throat chakra is the chakra between the heart chakra and the third-eye chakra, if our throat chakra has a lot of blockages from lies or secrets then our head and our hearts are not going to be working together when we make our choices. In energy medicine, this is called a split because the heart has no effect on the thinking going on in our brains, leaving our hearts and minds split from each other and the choices we make. Our thoughts can affect our biology quite literally by the messages and things we tell ourselves on a daily basis. When I started practicing affirmations and telling myself nice things about myself, I started feeling a lot better all over my body. Changing my thinking directly affected my physical health in really wonderful ways that I didn't realize was going to happen until I had changed my thinking for a couple of years.

Addiction is classified as a mental illness because it distorts and impairs the thinking of the person who is

Chapter Five — Consciously Choosing Life

addicted. This is another reason to strengthen the first chakra to get a really strong flow of energy that will help our brains, which are located in the area of the sixth chakra, to make good choices for us. Distorted thinking affects the perceptions and awareness of people who do not have a strong flow of energy coming to their sixth chakras. After we heal some of our original wounds, we are no longer controlled by the injuries and the choices we make because of the injuries and are able to independently make the most nourishing choices for ourselves and for others.

The sixth chakra is also connected to our dreams and the quality of the dreams we experience when we are sleeping. Deepak tells us that dreams bring us messages from our souls and that it is important to recapitulate our dreams in the morning when we wake up. I have seen many people who started working with their dreams on a regular basis begin to develop a lot of strong intuition and insights. This definitely started to happen to me as I continued working with my dreams over many years. I have had a few instances of dreaming about something and then finding the story from my dream on the front page of the newspaper that morning or walking into a store and finding a piece of clothing that was in my dream. I always read the entire story in the newspaper when this happens because it gives me a way to honor my dream, and I am also pretty certain that something in the article will be important to me and teach me something that will be useful to me down the road.

As part of my yoga training, I learned that there is "dream yoga," (42) and I was very excited to learn about this because I really like to work with my dreams and all of the many layers of meaning that come from them as well as the ways my dreams have connected me to other people in a way that would have never happened before.

The sixth chakra is connected to our eyes and how much of our spiritual essence shines or sparkles in our eyes, as well as the quality of our vision or perceptions about what we are taking in from our environment through our eyes. In Louie Schwartzberg's Youtube video

Chapter Five — Consciously Choosing Life

about gratitude, he talks about how 80 percent of what we take in from our environment is done visually, which makes our physical environments around us really important. The message we send with our physical appearance to others is also important because of how much information we all take in visually.

In ayurveda, we talk about two Sanskrit words: "ama" (toxic) and "ojas " (vitality and health). I also think of as ama as death or the worst in us and ojas as life or the best in us, and I think of many of my choices as choosing between life and death (or best and worst), and I want to choose life as often as possible. Choosing life brings many benefits to me physically, mentally, and spiritually and also helps spread life to others are around me. We make choices every day about whether we take in ama (worst) or ojas (best) with our eyes, and we make those same choices about whether we send out ama or ojas with our appearance. I am not an advocate of being dressed in high-fashion designer clothes every day, although I am an advocate of sending out ojas (best) with our appearance whenever possible. There are a number of ways to do this without spending a lot of money or time on getting dressed in the morning.

We become quite literally what we see unless we make conscious choices to surround ourselves with life-giving people and a life-giving physical environment. I included a series of pictures of how a small child can have very bright and sparkly eyes, be abused, and then have eyes that are dull and have less sparkle in them, and then as a young adult how this child is well on the way to looking like her mother (who has had a lot of soul loss), and then is able to get back to the original sparkly eyes by learning how to heal and retrieve the lost parts of her soul. (See Appendix A for these pictures.) This requires conscious choice making in all of the chakras, especially the first chakra, to have enough energy to keep working on this in spite of other people trying to discourage you because they want you to stay the same injured way.

We can also make the choice between ama (worst) and ojas (best) with our thoughts and what we choose to

Chapter Five — Consciously Choosing Life

spend our time thinking about as we go through our days and our lives. "Beauty is how you feel on the inside and it reflects in your eyes" (Sophia Loren). This is especially true when it comes to what we spend our time thinking about. The saying "energy flows where attention goes" is very true with our thoughts, and the things we spend the most time thinking about are what tend to grow in our lives, whether we are aware of it or not. In AA, they talk about "stinking thinking" and how thinking becomes distorted because of alcoholism and addiction. This is another reason the first chakra becomes vitally important so there is still a lot of energy coming into our brains to help us make quality choices to send out ojas and not get caught up in distorted thinking and misunderstandings.

Something I become more and more aware of as I work on my recovery is how many misunderstandings there are between people and how much difficulty this creates in relationships. I have seen this a number of times when people think they "know" something that upsets them and then they make cruel or destructive choices, and there has really been a misunderstanding between what they think they know and what the other person meant to communicate. Rather than risking being vulnerable and making sure they really understand something, they will jump to conclusions and make rash decisions that only make the situation worse instead of better. I have been really aware recently of how many misunderstandings there are between people and the harm that comes from this instead of making sure that both people are on the same page and understand what they mean before taking action.

"When we wake up to the fact that our thoughts touch the people we are thinking about, we are again asked to choose which thoughts we send out. If we send out the thoughts of the heart, we can heal, even if the person who needs healing is far away" (Robert Moss). (43) The quality of our thoughts as well as what we choose to think about become a very important choice between life and death when we spend a lot of our time thinking about the other people in our lives. We can have a positive or negative effect on others from a distance (ojas or ama), which is another reason to be more and more aware of what you spend your time thinking about and the quality of the thoughts you allow yourself to have.

Seventh Chakra

The seventh chakra is located at the top of the head and is known as the crown chakra. The crown chakra is our connection to spirit and a much more refined spiritual energy than the first chakra physical world. This is where we are able to look at the bigger picture and see ourselves as part of the one human race living on earth and how connected we are to each other just because we are all humans living on the same planet. The crown chakra contains our life lessons for this incarnation and is connected to our central nervous systems. Every experience we have is affected by the quality of our nervous systems and how we interpret the experience. Having a regular meditation practice helps soothe and calm our nervous systems, giving us much more acceptance of the way things are instead of getting angry that things are not the way we want them to be. This is also where we start to experience our oneness with all forms of life on earth. We are able to see that we all have the same mother—Mother Earth—and since we have the same mother, we are all related as one human race whether we realize it or not. We are all one divine species with the same mother in common. Chief Seattle was aware of this when he was talking about how we all share and breathe the same air. Having the same mother makes all of us part of the same family and just like smaller families, we get along better with some of our relatives than others.

"Learn how to see. Realize that everything connects to everything else" (Leonardo Da Vinci). (44) Evidently, Leonardo Da Vinci understood this connection between every living thing on the earth because of the one connection we all have to the one Mother Earth. It is amazing to me that, so many years later, much of the world's population appears to have not learned about the oneness of all life or learned a new way to see so they could

Chapter Five — Consciously Choosing Life

understand this connection that is there, whether they are aware of it or not.

Almost all of the major religions encourage and teach the importance of honoring your mother and father. In some families, like my ex-husband's family, the father teaches the children to treat their mother with disdain and disrespect so my ex-husband taught both of my children to treat me with disdain and disrespect. I believe that a lot of these children then treat our Mother Earth with disdain and disrespect by causing harm to the natural environment that we all share as living, breathing beings. It is important for all of us to work together to honor our one Mother Earth and treat her with respect and kindness. Mother Earth is really the "greatest" mother of all since she gives life to and supports life for more than seven billion people as well as all the plant and animal kingdoms. It is time for us to come together and find ways to nurture and sustain our Mother Earth.

Having a regular meditation practice changes our vibrations and the types of people and circumstances we

I Choose Life

attract to us. "Everything is energy and that is all there is to it. Match the frequency of the reality you want and you cannot help but get that reality" (Albert Einstein). (45) When we change our vibrations and energy fields, we are able to heal the injuries we have received during our lifetimes so that the damage doesn't control us, or the choices we make anymore. When one person changes, he or she has already started to change the world. Many advanced yogis acquire siddhis (spiritual powers) over many years of regular practice of meditation and yoga. Once they acquire these powers, they will never misuse them and will only use them for the benefit of others. We all benefit from these yogis because just their presence is healing to anyone around them due to the energy and vibration fields they have built up around them.

"It is not about changing your colors; it is about the transformation of the soul and the ability to become one with all of the beauty that surrounds you" (Mystic Amari). (46) This is what happens when we start making the small changes that help bring balance to each of our

Chapter Five — Consciously Choosing Life

chakras; then we are able to see all of the beauty around us and in others around us, and we realize that by nurturing and being true to ourselves, we become Be.YOU.tiful inside and out and are able to celebrate and be aware of that same beauty in others around us.

"Array thyself with glory and beauty" (Job 40:10). "Worship the Lord in beauty" (Psalm 29:2). These verses made me wonder if this is why so many Protestant churches talk about and have the practice of wearing your "Sunday best" and dressing very nicely to go to church because that was their understanding of these verses. What if the message was to worship God by being you and arraying yourself in the glory and the beauty of being yourself 100 percent in each of your chakras and your being? What if this was the real beauty God wants us to nurture and develop within ourselves? I think we have all met people who had on beautiful clothing, but their insides were not beautiful, and so the beautiful clothing didn't really matter because we could feel the inauthenticity of the person no matter what clothing they were wearing. What if real worship is to honor and develop the beauty within each one of us? What if loving and accepting ourselves—our physical bodies, our emotions, our skills and abilities, our hopes and dreams, our desires—is how we really worship God and become more Be.YOU.tiful the more we really love everything about us and love being ourselves?

"Every moment, a new beauty" (Rumi). (47) In every moment, we have the opportunity to be our true authentic selves and to honor and respect this in other people. When we really start to nurture this in ourselves, we are able to see the real beauty in the other people around us and have acceptance for all members of humanity and all life forms just the way they are. We start to experience more unity in our whole beings because our chakras are strong and functioning as one "united" group instead of being fragmented or split from each other, and this is where the real unity begins—within ourselves and our chakras. Then we can experience this unity and union with others around us.

Chapter Five — Consciously Choosing Life

Heaven on Earth

Another interesting aspect of the chakras as a group is that some of them are paired together and affect each other. Chakras one (body), Four (mind – Chinese medicine), and seven (spirit) are all connected to each other. Chakras two and five are connected to each other. Chakras three and six are connected to each other.

"That ye, being rooted and grounded in love, may be able to comprehend and be filled with all the fullness of God" (Ephesians 3:17-19). This verse fascinates me because it illustrates the connection between chakras one, four, and seven. When we are firmly grounded in our first chakras and able to give and receive love in our fourth chakras then we are able to comprehend and be filled with the fullness of God (heaven) in our seventh chakras. In some way, Paul understood this connection between our roots and our hearts and our ability to connect to spirit and the oneness and unity that is all around us. I believe he was giving us instructions for how we can experience *"Heaven on Earth."* This verse is part of the inspiration for this book because when we are grounded and connected to our bodies, communities and families, giving and receiving love in our fourth chakras (our real minds)—especially loving ourselves and our own unique individual expressions—and connected to spirit in our seventh chakras and are able to embrace and incorporate Deepak Chopra's seven spiritual laws (48) in our daily lives then we are able to experience *Heaven on Earth* in our everyday lives. We can *Choose Life, One, Two, Three* by practicing these three things every day.

Abundant Life

"I am come that they might have life, and that they might have it more abundantly" (John 10:10). I think that Jesus was promising us this experience of *Heaven on Earth* in this verse and letting us know that this is possible in our physical bodies, and we don't need to wait until we die to experience abundant life here on earth.

The connection between our second and fifth chakras is important because our ability to relate to others is directly affected by our ability to communicate to others what our needs, wants, interests, and intentions are. It is especially important when we remember that the second chakra is the seat of most addictions and how that affects what comes out of our mouths and whether we tell the truth or lies to other people. It is also important because the words we hear around us can trigger powerful emotions within us, and this affects the reactions we will have to the words we hear.

The connection between our third and sixth chakras is important because our ability to stand in our own power and be nonjudgmental of others affects our thinking and perceptions of what is going on around us. Our interpretations and thinking about situations are directly influenced by our self-esteem and confidence in ourselves to accomplish things in the world. I have heard it said that the most judgmental people are the ones with low self-esteem. When we don't feel good about ourselves or have a lot of shame we are carrying around with us, we aren't able to easily have positive thinking and thoughts most of the time.

All of the chakras are connected and are part of the same system, and achieving unity within the chakra system is really the first step toward achieving unity in the world around us. This is really what the practice of yoga is all about, as well as achieving balance in each chakra.

Communities of Love

"It is the waves of Love that turn the wheels of Heaven; without Love, nothing would have life" (Rumi). (49) We can have communities of support to help us manifest *Heaven on Earth* by focusing on generating and sending out waves of love instead of the pain and agony of addiction. We can work together to provide nurturing and safe environments for our children to grow up in. We can teach children to honor and embrace their own unique fingerprints as they are growing up. We can help children learn to share their fingerprints by sharing their piece of Divine love with the world in a healthy way. We can teach our children financial life skills as well as other life skills so they feel strong and secure within themselves and

Chapter Five — Consciously Choosing Life

their abilities to provide for themselves. We can teach our children to send out God's kisses to the world by saying their "OM's" every day. We can support each other on our journeys through life and whatever challenges come our way.

One Song by Rumi(50)

Every war and every conflict between human beings has happened, because of some disagreement about names.

It is such an unnecessary foolishness, because just beyond the arguing, there is a long table of companionship set and waiting for us to sit down.

What is praised is One, so the praise is one too,

Many jugs being poured into a huge basin.

All religions, all this singing, One Song.

The differences are just illusion and vanity.

Sunlight looks a little different on this wall than it does on that wall,

And a lot different on this other one, but it is still One light.

I Choose Life

We have borrowed these clothes, these time-and-space personalities, from a light, and when we praise, we are pouring them back in.

We are all a part of the same song regardless of the names or words we use to express our worldviews. Every living thing has the same mother earth in common, the same song in common, and the same family in common and once we really understand, accept and integrate that into our beings, our lives start to give us the experience of *Heaven on Earth*.

One definition of heaven is a state or a place of blessed existence. We can send out the waves of love from our communities of love to create a place of blessed existence around us, and we don't have to die before we can begin to experience this. In the dream work tradition of Robert Moss, if I were going to write a bumper sticker to summarize this book, it would be: "Get Grounded for Life and Experience *Heaven on Earth*."

Appendix A — Pictures of the physical changes due to soul loss

Appendix B — Positive Words and Traits

"Your task is not to seek love, but merely to seek and find all the barriers within yourself that you have built against it."—Rumi (51)

Aloha

Admirable

Awesome

Attentive

I Choose Life

Alive	Abundant
Adorable	All right
Alert	Aware
Assertive	Am
Accountable	
Awake	Beautiful
Amazing	Bright
Accepting	Brave
Attractive	Brilliant
Articulate	Best
Artistic	Becoming
Authentic	Bold
Appropriate	Bountiful
Approachable	Balanced
Appreciative	Benevolent
Affectionate	Beaming
Active	Blessed
Able	
Agreeable	Cute
Accomplished	Calm

Appendix B — Positive Words and Traits

Curious
Celebrate
Courageous
Contagious
Charming
Clever
Cheerful
Capable
Careful
Cautious
Complex
Connected
Consistent
Comical
Comforting
Creative
Caring
Confident
Competent
Civilized

Complete
Child of God
Considerate
Compassionate
Contributing
Collaborative
Conscientious

a Dancer
Dynamite
Delightful
Dedicated
Devoted
Dear
Dynamic
Determined
Daring
Darling
Dutiful
Delicious

Deserving
Discerning
Durable
Divine
Dreamer
Diligent
Dainty
Desirable
Dependable

Eternal
Evolving
Enough
Emotional
Endearing
Employable
Even-tempered
Energetic
Excellent
Ecstasy

Euphoric
Expressive
Engaging
Exquisite
Exemplary
Exciting
Exceptional
Earnest
Enterprising
Enchanting
Enjoyable
Endurance
Encouraging
Efficient
Entertaining
Enthusiastic
Effective
Empathetic
Experienced
Empowered

Appendix B — Positive Words and Traits

Effervescent

Extraordinary

Exuberant

Fun/funny

Fantastic

Fabulous

Friendly

Fearless

Faithful

Fanciful

Fashionable

Fast

Flexible

Famous

Fit

Fulfilled

Focused

Frugal

Free

Fortuitous

Fresh

Glowing

Glorious

Grateful

Glamorous

Great

Gracious

Giving

Grace-filled

Generous

Gifted

Gorgeous

Genuine

Girly

Gregarious

Gentle

Grounded

Helpful	Informed
Honest	Impressive
Hardworking	Intelligent
Heroic	Introspective
Healthy	Interesting
Happy	Intuitive
"Hot"	Inventive
Humorous	Intriguing
Healer	Insightful
Honorable	Industrious
Hope/hopeful	Illuminating
Honorable	Infinite
Harmonizing	Invincible
Handsome	Independent
Hilarious	Indispensable
Helper	Impeccable
Humble	Influential
Holy	Integrity
Healthy	Inspirational
	Invigorating

Appendix B — Positive Words and Traits

Irresistible

Incredible

Inspiring

Important

Insightful

Jovial

Judicious

Joyful

Jubilant

Jolly

Joking

Just

Kind

Knowledgeable

Knack-ful

Kindred

Kooky

Kazowie

Kissable

Lucky

Loving

Loyal

Likable

Laughing

Life-giving

Limitless

Lively

Lovable

Lighthearted

Luscious

Lustrous

Lovable

Learned

Loyal

Listener

Loved

Learning every day

I Choose Life

Life	Masterful
Light	Monumental
	Marvelous
Motivated	Masterpiece
Ministering	
Mature	Nice
Magnificent	Neat
Magnanimous	Noticeable
Mindful	Nurturing
Merciful	Noble
Merry	Natural
Motherly	Nourishing
Melodious	Nifty
Meticulous	New
Magical	Neighborly
Memorable	
Me	Organized
Matter	Open
Musical	Open-minded
Miraculous	Optimistic

Appendix B — Positive Words and Traits

One of a kind
Original
Outgoing
Opulent
Observant
Okay

Polite
Passionate
Potential
Popular
Progressive
Positive
Patient
Productive
Pretty
Peaceful
Pleasant
Precious
Perceptive

Protective
Perseverant
Present
Polished
Praiseworthy
Practical
Punctual
Powerful
Protective
Principled
a Phoenix
Playful
Pure potential

Quiet
Quality
Questioning
Quirky
Quick
Quaint

I Choose Life

Responsible	Responsible
Real	
Reflective	Significant
Realistic	Spectacular
Reasonable	Sweet
Resourceful	Sincere
Ravishing	Sympathetic
Right	Smart
Radiant	Sensational
Relevant	Super
Reassuring	Splendid
Relaxed	Sensitive
Romantic	Social
Respected	Satisfied
Restored	Soothing
Reliable	Spiritual
Rare	Stable
Remarkable	*Special delivery*
Rosy	Strong
Rested	Smiley

Appendix B — Positive Words and Traits

Saintly
Selective
Sunny
Stylish
Successful
Serene
Simple
Smashing
Sleek
Swift
Safe
Silly
Studious
Secure
Sharing
Scientific
Serenity
Special
Supporting/Supportive

Talented
Transformational
Trustworthy
Tremendous
Terrific
Truthful
Thoughtful
Thankful
Tough
Teachable
Timeless
Tenacious
Team player
Tender
Tried and true
Thorough
Tolerant
Thrifty
Touching
Trim

Universal
Unique
Understanding
Unbelievable
Uplifting
Unity
Useful
Unparalleled
Unbounded

Vivacious
Vital
Vibrant
Valuable
Volunteer
Victorious
Vulnerable

Wonderful
Willing

Wise
Whimsical
Winning
Worthy
Watchful
Wholesome
Winner
Wow
Witty
Washed
Whole
Warm
Worthwhile
Wisdom
Wanted
a Work of Art

Youthful
Young at heart
Yummy

Appendix B — Positive Words and Traits

Yowza	Zowie
Yes	Zealous
Yielding	Zestful
Yahoo	

I Choose Life

Endnotes:

1. Facebook page: Rumi quotes, photos section
2. *11:11* by Solara, 1992
3. *Symphonia: A Critical Edition of the "Symphonia Armonie Celestium Revelationum" (Symphony of the Harmony of Celestial Revelations)*, Hildegard of Bingen (Author), Barbara Newman (Translator), published 1988, 1998
4. *The Joy in Loving: Daily Wisdom with Mother Teresa*, published 1997
5. OWN (Oprah Winfrey Network) Facebook page from Super Soul Sunday, Season 3, Episode with Iyanla Vanzant
6. OWN (Oprah Winfrey Network) Facebook page from Super Soul Sunday, Episode with Three New Faces that originally aired 11/18/2012

7. You Can Heal Your Life by Louise Hay, published 1999

8. Oprah.com website; article on "Male Sexual Abuse Survivors Stand Together," published Nov. 5, 2010

9. *The Artist's Way* by Jullia Cameron, published 1992, 2002

10. *Disciple: Becoming Disciples Through Bible Study* by Richard B. Wilke and Julia K. Wilke, Study Manual published 1987, Second Edition published 1993

11. *Christian Believer: Knowing God with Heart and Mind* by J. Ellsworth Kalas, published 1999

12. Institute of Heartmath, www.heartmath.org, Articles of the Heart, Section Titled Power of the Heart's Electromagnetic Field and 2008 Global Coherence Initiative

13. OWN (Oprah Winfrey Network) Facebook page from Super Soul Sunday Episode aired 3/17/2013

14. Facebook page: Rumi quotes, photos section

15. *The Healing Path of Prayer: A Modern Mystic's Guide to Spiritual Power* by Ron Roth, Ph.D. and Peter Occhiogrosso, published 1998

Endnotes

16. *A Paramhansa Yogananda Trilogy of Divine Love* by Sri Durga Mata, published 1992 by Joan Wright
17. *Conscious Dreaming: A Spiritual Path for Everyday Life* by Robert Moss, published 1996
18. *Joan of Arc: The Warrior Saint* by Stephen W. Richey, published October 2003
19. *Sitting Bull and the Paradox of Lakota Nationhood* by Gary C. Anderson, published April 2006, Second Edition
20. *Cloud Atlas,* starring Tom Hanks and Halle Berry, released 2012 by Warner Bros. Entertainment
21. *The Joy in Loving: Daily Wisdom with Mother Teresa,* published 1997
22. *Everything Starts from Prayer; Mother Teresa's Meditations on Spiritual Life for People of All Faiths* by Anthony Stern, M.D., published 1998
23. *Perfect Health: The Complete Mind Body Guide* by Deepak Chopra, M.D., published 1991, 2000
24. *A Year with Rumi Daily Readings* by Coleman Barks, published 2006, November 22, page 366

I Choose Life

25. Facebook page: Paramahansa Yogananda
26. Facebook page: Paramahansa Yogananda
27. Bravo TV Show, "Project Runway," First Season, 2004
28. *The Seven Spiritual Laws of Yoga* by Deepak Chopra, M.D., and David Simon, M.D., published 2004
29. Facebook page: The Afterlife of Billy Fingers, photos section
30. Facebook page: Rumi quotes, photos section
31. Website: www.brainyquote.com, quote by Ossie Davis, actor
32. Institute of Heartmath, www.heartmath.org, Articles of the Heart, Section Titled Power of the Heart's Electromagnetic Field and 2008 Global Coherence Initiative
33. Institute of Noetic Sciences, located in Petaluma, CA, website: www.noetic.org
34. Facebook page: Spirit science and metaphysics, photos section
35. Facebook Page: Rumi Quotes, photos section

Endnotes

36. *The Three Only Things: Tapping the Power of Dreams, Coincidence and Imagination* by Robert Moss, published 2007, pages 66-67
37. Facebook page: Rumi quotes, photos section
38. Facebook page: Osho quotes, photos section
39. Facebook page: Rumi quotes, photos section
40. Website for Masaru Emoto Peace Project is www.emoto-peace-project.com. Project announced at the Spiritual Dimensions of Science and Consciousness Subcommittee at United Nation Headquarter in NYC on May 25, 2005
41. OWN (Oprah Winfrey Network) Facebook post from Super Soul Sunday, show aired on 5/12/13 with Maya Angelou
42. *Realities of the Dreaming Mind: The Practice of Dream Yoga* by Swami Sivananda Radha, published 2004
43. *Dreamways of the Iroquois Honoring the Secret Wishes of the Soul* by Robert Moss, published 2004, page 159
44. Facebook page: Spirit science and metaphysics, photos section

I Choose Life

45. Facebook page: Albert Einstein Facebook quotes, photos section
46. Facebook page: Mystic Amari, photos section
47. Facebook page: Rumi quotes, photos section
48. *The Seven Spiritual Laws of Success* by Deepak Chopra, M.D., published 1994, abridged edition 2007
49. Facebook page: Rumi quotes, photos section
50. Facebook page: Rumi quotes, "One Song" poem at top of home page
51. Facebook page: Rumi quotes, photos section

Endnotes

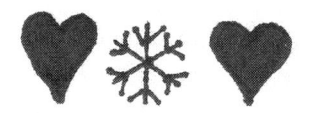

The author can be contacted at the following email address: bgodskissdaley@aol.com